Series Editors:
Carollee Howes
Robert C. Pianta

ncrece
national center for research on early childhood education
SERIES

Foundations for
Teaching Excellence

Also in the *National Center for Research on Early Childhood Education Series:*

The Promise of Pre-K
edited by Robert C. Pianta, Ph.D.,
and Carollee Howes, Ph.D.

SERIES

Foundations for Teaching Excellence

Connecting Early Childhood Quality Rating, Professional Development, and Competency Systems in States

Carollee Howes, Ph.D.
University of California, Los Angeles

and

Robert C. Pianta, Ph.D.
University of Virginia, Charlottesville

·P A U L·H·
BROOKES
PUBLISHING Cº ®

Baltimore • London • Sydney

Paul H. Brookes Publishing Co.
Post Office Box 10624
Baltimore, Maryland 21285-0624
USA

www.brookespublishing.com

Typeset by Aptara, Inc., Falls Church, Virginia.
Manufactured in the United States of America by
Versa Press, Inc., East Peoria, Illinois.

The individuals described in this book are composites or real people whose situations
are masked and are based on the authors' experiences. In all instances, names and
identifying details have been changed to protect confidentiality.

The publisher and the authors have made every effort to ensure that all the information in
this book is as accurate as possible at the time of press; given the changing nature of the
information, future authenticity or reliability cannot be guaranteed. Updates for corrections
or changes may be submitted to the publisher for consideration in future printings.

Supported in part by the Institute of Education Sciences, U.S. Department of Education,
through Grant R305A060021 to the University of Virginia. However, the content does not
necessarily reflect the position of the U.S. Department of Education, and no official
endorsement should be inferred.

Library of Congress Cataloging-in-Publication Data

Foundations for teaching excellence: connecting early childhood quality rating,
professional development, and competency systems in states / [edited by] Carollee Howes,
Robert C. Pianta; with invited contributors.
    p.   cm.—(National Center for Research on Early Childhood Education series)
    Includes bibliographical references and index.
    ISBN-13: 978-1-59857-122-6
    ISBN-10: 1-59857-122-2
    1. Early childhood teachers—In-service training—United States—States.   2. Early
childhood teachers—Rating of—United States—States.   3. Early childhood education—
United States—States.   I. Howes, Carollee.   II. Pianta, Robert C.
    LB1775.6.F68   2010
    372.11—dc22   2010023178

2014   2013   2012   2011   2010

10   9   8   7   6   5   4   3   2   1

Contents

I National-Level Concerns

II Implementation at the State Level

Series Preface

The National Center for Research on Early Childhood Education (NCRECE) series on the future of early childhood education addresses key topics related to improving the quality of early childhood education in the United States. Each volume is a culmination of presentations and discussions taking place during the annual NCRECE Leadership Symposium, which brings together leaders and stakeholders in the field to discuss and synthesize the current knowledge about prominent issues that affect the educational experiences and outcomes of young children. Most important, it is the aim of these symposia, and the related series volumes, to be forward looking, identifying nascent topics that have the potential for improving the quality of early childhood education and then defining, analyzing, and charting conceptual, policy, practice, and research aims for the future. Topics to be addressed in subsequent volumes include the nature and quality of publicly funded preschool programs and the integration of quality rating systems, early childhood competencies, and models of professional development.

The series is designed to stimulate critical thinking around these key topics and to help inform future research agendas. The series should be of interest to a broad range of researchers, policy makers, teacher educators, and practitioners.

Carollee Howes, Ph.D.
Robert C. Pianta, Ph.D.

About the Editors

Carollee Howes, Ph.D., is Director of the Center for Improving Child Care Quality, Department of Education, and a professor of the applied developmental doctorate program at the University of California, Los Angeles (UCLA). Dr. Howes is an internationally recognized developmental psychologist focusing on children's social and emotional development. She has served as a principal investigator on a number of seminal studies in early child care and preschool education, including the National Child Care Staffing Study; the Family and Relative Care Study; the Cost, Quality, and Outcomes Study; and the National Study of Child Care in Low Income Families. Dr. Howes has been active in public policy for children and families in California as well as across the United States. Her research focuses on children's experiences in child care, their concurrent and long-term outcomes from child care experiences, and child care quality and efforts to improve child care quality. Dr. Howes is the author of *Teaching 4- to 8-Year-Olds: Literacy, Math, Multiculturalism, and Classroom Community* (Paul H. Brookes Publishing Co., 2003).

Robert C. Pianta, Ph.D., is Dean of the Curry School of Education, Novartis US Foundation Professor of Education, Director of the National Center for Research on Early Childhood Education (NCRECE), and Director of the Center for Advanced Study of Teaching and Learning (CASTL) at the University of Virginia, Charlottesville. A former special education teacher, Dr. Pianta is particularly interested in how relationships with teachers and parents as well as classroom experiences can help improve outcomes for at-risk children and youth. Dr. Pianta in a principal investigator on several major grants, including MyTeachingPartner, the Institute of Education Sciences Interdisciplinary Doctoral Training Program in Risk and Prevention, and the National Institute of Child Health and Human Development (NICHD) Study of Early Child Care and Youth Development (SECCYD). He was also a senior investigator for the National Center for Early Development and Learning (NCEDL) and served as Editor of the *Journal of School Psychology*. He is the author of more than 300 journal articles, chapters, and books in the areas of early childhood development, transition to school, school readiness, and parent–child and teacher–child relationships, including *The Promise of Pre-K* (coedited with Carollee Howes, Paul H. Brookes Publishing Co., 2009), *School Readiness and the Transition to Kindergarten in the Era of Accountability* (coedited with Martha J. Cox and Kyle L. Snow, Paul H. Brookes Publishing Co., 2007), and *Classroom Assessment Scoring System* (CLASS; coauthored with Karen M. La Paro and Bridget K. Hamre, Paul H. Brookes Publishing Co., 2008). Dr. Pianta consults regularly with federal agencies, foundations, and universities.

About the Contributors

Barbara Coccodrilli Carlson, J.D., M.A., State Technical Assistance Specialist, Region II, National Child Care Information and Technical Assistance Center, 10530 Rosehaven Street, Suite 400, Fairfax, Virginia 22030

Ms. Carlson is State Technical Assistance Specialist, Region II, for the National Child Care Information and Technical Assistance Center of Fairfax, Virginia, and has worked for 30 years in the areas of child and family policy as a teacher, attorney, policy analyst, advocate, strategic planner, and foundation executive. Ms. Carlson has been affiliated with the Child Care Law Center; the Carnegie Corporation; the National Center for Law and Economic Justice; the NYS Council on Children and Families; and the San Francisco Mayor's Office of Children, Youth and Families. Ms. Carlson was the founding director of Early Childhood Programs at the Miriam and Peter Haas Fund and the founding executive director of the NYC Early Childhood Professional Development Institute.

Lori Connors-Tadros, Ph.D., Vice President, Children and Family Services, The Finance Project, 1401 New York Avenue NW, Suite 800, Washington, D.C. 20005

Dr. Connors-Tadros is Vice President, Children and Family Services with The Finance Project in Washington, D.C., and works with state and local leaders to support decision making and develop solutions for financing and sustaining early care and education, out-of-school time, youth development, and other services supporting children and families. She also has more than 30 years experience in the fields of education and psychology. Prior to joining The Finance Project, she worked for the National Child Care Information Center supporting state efforts to improve the quality of child care for low-income parents and to implement federal policies related to early learning and school readiness.

Jerlean E. Daniel, Ph.D., Executive Director, National Association for the Education of Young Children, 1313 L Street NW, Suite 500, Washington D.C. 20005

Dr. Daniel is the Executive Director of the National Association for the Education of Young Children in Washington, D.C., and has served young children and their families in a variety of capacities for more than 40 years. After 18 years as a child care center director, she served as faculty and department chair at the University of Pittsburgh, preparing undergraduates and graduate students for careers focused on the development of children and youth.

Jill Haak, M.Ed., University of Virginia, Center for Advanced Study of Teaching and Learning, 350 Old Ivy Way, Suite 100, Charlottesville, Virginia 22903

Ms. Haak is a doctoral student in the Clinical and School Psychology programs in the Curry School of Education at the University of Virginia. Ms. Haak conducted research on early childhood education and development at the Center for Advanced Study of Teaching and Learning at the University of Virginia. She is specifically interested in behavioral and academic outcomes related to home preliteracy and promoting positive social and emotional development in early childhood through teacher and parent training.

Tamara Halle, Ph.D., Director of Early Learning and Transition to School, Child Trends, 4301 Connecticut Avenue NW, Suite 350, Washington, D.C. 20008

Dr. Halle is Director of Early Learning and Transition to School at Child Trends. Dr. Halle conducts research on children's early cognitive and social development, children's school readiness, and school characteristics associated with ongoing achievement and positive development. Her recent work focuses especially on early literacy development among English language learning children and evaluations of early childhood curricula, programs, and professional development aimed at supporting children's school readiness. She received her doctorate in developmental psychology from the University of Michigan.

Sandra L. Soliday Hong, M.Ed., University of California, Los Angeles, Center for Improving Child Care Quality, Graduate School of Education and Information Studies, 8118 Math Sciences Building, Box 951521, Los Angeles, California 90095-1521

Ms. Hong is a doctoral candidate at the University of California, Los Angeles (UCLA), and her interests include child care quality, teaching, and children's social and emotional development. Ms. Hong is a former early childhood teacher and is currently working on the Steps to Excellence Project to improve child care quality in Los Angeles through the Center for Improving Child Care Quality at UCLA.

Youngok Jung, M.Ed., M.A., University of California, Los Angeles, 8118 Math Sciences Building, Box 951521, Los Angeles, California 90095-1521

Ms. Jung is a doctoral candidate at the University of California, Los Angeles.

Sarah LeMoine, M.S., Director, Early Child Workforce Systems Initiative, National Association for the Education of Young Children (NAEYC), 1313 L Street NW, Suite 500, Washington, D.C. 20005-4101

Ms. LeMoine is the Director of the Early Childhood Workforce Systems Initiative at the National Association for the Education of Young Children. Since the early 1980s, Ms. LeMoine has worked to support high-quality education a care for all young children, with a primary focus on early childhood professional development systems and activities, workforce diversity, and leadership issues. The Initiative's purpose is to assist states in developing, enhancing, and implementing policies for an integrated early childhood professional development system—a system serving all early childhood education professionals working with and on behalf of young children.

Alison Lutton, M.S., Senior Director of the Higher Education Accreditation and Program Support at the National Association for the Education of Young Children (NAEYC), 1313 L Street NW, Suite 500, Washington, D.C. 20005-4101

Ms. Lutton is Senior Director of the Higher Education Accreditation and Program Support at the National Association for the Education of Young Children (NAEYC), and has more than 30 years' experience working in early childhood education. Her direct work with children includes residential and educational programs for children with severe disabilities and family child care. After 15 years as early childhood faculty at the Community College of Philadelphia and at Northampton Community College in Bethlehem, Pennsylvania, Ms. Lutton joined NAEYC in 2006. She is currently the Senior Director of Higher Education Accreditation and Support at NAEYC.

Davida McDonald, M.P.H., Director of State Policy at the National Association for the Education of Young Children (NAEYC), 1313 L Street NW, Suite 500, Washington, D.C. 20005-4101

Ms. McDonald is Director of State Policy at the National Association for the Education of Young Children (NAEYC), where her primary responsibilities are researching and tracking state public policy trends and working with state and local affiliates to build their public policy capacity. Ms. McDonald brings to NAEYC a knowledge of statewide advocacy and coalition-building campaigns.

Tamar Mintz, M.Ed., University of Virginia, Curry School of Education, Clinical and School Psychology, 405 Emmet Street, Charlottesville, Virginia 22903

Ms. Mintz received her undergraduate degree from Brandeis University and is a doctoral student in clinical and school psychology at the University of Virginia. Her interests include family factors that contribute to children's school success in the transition to school, interventions for at-risk children, and children's social and emotional development.

Kathryn Tout, Ph.D., Director of Applied Research in Early Care and Education at Child Trends, 615 First Avenue, NE, Suite 225, Minneapolis, Minnesota 55413

Dr. Tout is the Director of Applied Research in Early Care and Education at Child Trends and oversees projects in Child Trends's Minnesota office. Her research focuses on policies and programs to improve the quality of early care and education as well as families' access to quality settings, and programs to improve the quality and effectiveness of the early childhood workforce.

Catherine Tsao, M.A., University of California, Los Angeles (UCLA), Graduate School of Education and Information Studies, 8118 Math Sciences Building, Box 951521, Los Angeles, California 90095-1521

Ms. Tsao is a doctoral student at the University of California, Los Angeles (UCLA) Graduate School of Education and Information Studies. Her research interests include socioemotional development in children from birth to 5 years of age and child care quality. Her previous experience includes administration of a university-based infant-toddler lab school, undergraduate instruction, and work in educational policy.

Promjawan Udommana, M.A., University of California, Los Angeles (UCLA), Graduate School of Education and Information Studies, 8118 Math Sciences Building, Box 951521, Los Angeles, California 90095-1521

Ms. Udommana is a doctoral student at the University of California, Los Angeles (UCLA). Her research focuses on early care and education experience of children of Thai immigrants in the United States and child care quality in Thailand.

Jennifer Vu, Ph.D., Assistant Professor, Human Development and Family Studies, University of Delaware, 126 Alison Hall South, Newark, Delaware 19716

Dr. Vu is Assistant Professor in the Department of Human Development and Family Studies at the University of Delaware. Her areas of research interest include child care quality and professional development as well as young children's socioemotional development.

Terri Walters, M.A.T., University of Virginia, 350 Old Ivy Way, Suite 100, Charlottesville, Virginia 22903

Ms. Walters is a doctoral student at the University of Virginia. Before attending graduate school, she was a first-grade teacher.

Debra Weinstein, M.S.W., Research Assistant, Child Trends, 4301 Connecticut Avenue NW, Suite 350, Washington, D.C. 20008

Tracey West, Ph.D., Social Research Specialist, Frank Porter Graham Child Development Institute, Campus Box 8185, The University of North Carolina, Chapel Hill, North Carolina 27599-8185

Dr. West is the Coordinator of the National Professional Development Center on Inclusion. Dr. West completed her doctoral degree in Early Childhood, Families, and Literacy at The University of North Carolina at Chapel Hill. Her research interests are in early childhood and inclusion.

Pamela J. Winton, Ph.D., Senior Scientist and Director of Outreach at the Frank Porter Graham Child Development Institute, Campus Box 8185, The University of North Carolina, Chapel Hill, North Carolina 27599-8185

Dr. Winton is Senior Scientist and Director of Outreach at the Frank Porter Graham Child Development Institute at The University of North Carolina at Chapel Hill. Dr. Winton has been involved in research, outreach, and professional development related to early childhood since the mid-1980s, including directing federally funded national centers, publishing books, and involvement on eleven different federally funded early childhood research institutes and projects, including directing six as either principal investigator or co-principal investigator.

Martha Zaslow, Ph.D., is Director of the Office for Policy and Communications of the Society for Research in Child Development and a Senior Scholar at Child Trends, a nonpartisan, nonprofit research organization in

Washington, D.C., that focuses on research and statistics on children and families in the United States. Dr. Zaslow received her doctoral degree in personality and developmental psychology from Harvard University, Cambridge, Massachusetts, and her research focuses on early childhood development taking an ecological approach, considering the role of multiple contexts, including the family, early care and education settings, and programs and policies for families with young children. She is especially interested in understanding how to strengthen quality in early care and education settings and in how children's experiences in such settings contribute to school readiness.

Foreword

The professional development of our nation's early childhood workforce has been put in the spotlight in recent years as a result of increased public and private funding, an expansion of early childhood education (ECE) programs serving our youngest children, and the implementation of both targeted and systemic approaches to improve the quality of those programs. Scrutiny of ECE professional development, as most commonly delivered, has resulted from the realization that assumptions held by the field of early care and education about the positive links between levels of formal education (including terminal degrees), certification, and training received by teachers and caregivers, on the one hand, and children's outcomes in key developmental domains, on the other, are not fully supported by recent research evidence. In addition, as pointed out by authors in this volume, states and localities are developing and implementing new systems to align governance, standards, financing, communication, and accountability systems of ECE programs (e.g., quality rating and improvement systems), underscoring the urgent need to strengthen professional development as currently delivered.

Why do we need to revisit our current approaches to professional development of the ECE workforce? Findings from recent research to assess the effectiveness of professional development models in improving the quality of ECE programs, including practices known to support children's development, show significant improvements in process quality and practices, but only when those models have included innovations such as coaching and mentoring that are not normally implemented in our current approaches to the delivery of professional development (e.g., coursework accompanied by on-site coaching, training in curricula paired with coaching; Layzer, Layzer, Goodson, & Price, 2009; Neuman & Cunningham, 2009). In addition, meta-analyses and secondary analyses of data from observational assessments of quality in center-based ECE programs and from child assessments in different developmental domains are showing modest associations between structural features of quality, such as levels of education, degrees, and certificates, and children's outcomes, findings that call into question the ability of current efforts to train and educate our ECE workforce to produce the practices that are linked to children's development (Burchinal et al., 2009). The available research evidence is insufficient, however, to help us determine with confidence which specific practices in ECE programs, both in centers and homes, are providing the supports our children need to develop the skills that will help them succeed in school and in life. Among the practices that stand in need of further research and evaluation are those which address the unique needs of children of different ages, children with different cultural and language backgrounds, and children with unique special needs.

Achieving the goal of supporting young children's early learning and development is at the center of many current federal and state policies for ECE programs and interventions and is especially critical for those programs serving young children from low-income households and with multiple risk factors. New federal research investments are addressing gaps in our understanding of the features, thresholds, and "dosages" of quality that are necessary to benefit children's development. The ultimate goal is to inform the design of quality initiatives that will focus on improving practice in ECE programs (in particular, those initiatives focused on professional development) and the quality of interactions between teachers and caregivers and the children in their care. Recent efforts to revamp professional development systems have focused on multiple components of these systems, such as 1) strengthening the content of training and coursework in order to build foundational knowledge on the developmental trajectories of children, good pedagogy in early childhood, and ways to adapt practices to the specific needs of diverse children in different types of ECE programs (Zaslow & Martinez-Beck, 2005); 2) aligning professional development standards and required competencies across delivery methods, including preservice and in-service training, coursework leading to certificates and degrees, and other targeted one-to-one efforts to change practice; and 3) developing workforce and professional development data systems (e.g., registries) for tracking and managing the implementation of professional development efforts.

The chapters in this volume have the potential to make a large contribution to local, state, and national discussions related to improvements in the design and delivery of professional development approaches as well as professional development systems. There seems to be a rising consensus in the field of early childhood studies that supporting the development of competencies and practices of early childhood practitioners may be the best avenue to improve the quality of ECE programs, thus increasing the likelihood that our young children will arrive in school with the knowledge, skills, and dispositions necessary to advance and succeed. The task ahead is not simple or easy and requires careful reexamination of our current approaches to professional development and the desire and will to implement large changes.

Ivelisse Martinez-Beck, Ph.D.
Senior Social Science Research Analyst
and Child Care Research Coordinator
Office of Planning, Research and Evaluation
Administration for Children and Families

REFERENCES

Burchinal, M., Kainz, K., Cai, K., Tout, K., Martinez-Beck, I., & Rathgeb, C. (2009, May). *Early care and education quality and child outcomes.* Washington, DC: U.S. Department of Health and Human Services, Administration for Children and Families, Office of Planning, Research and Evaluation.

Layzer, J., Layzer, C., Goodson, B., & Price, C. (2009, January). *Project Upgrade: Evaluation of child care subsidy strategies—Findings from an experimental evaluation of three language/literacy interventions in child care centers in Miami-Dade county.* Washington, DC: U.S. Department of Health and Human Services, Administration for Children and Families, Office of Planning, Research and Evaluation.

Neuman, S., & Cunningham, L. (2009). The impact of professional development and coaching on early language and literacy instruction. *American Educational Research Journal, 46*(2), 532–566.

Zaslow, M., & Martinez-Beck, I. (Eds.). (2005). *Critical issues in early childhood professional development.* Baltimore: Paul H. Brookes Publishing Co.

Preface

Policy makers, educators, and researchers have long assumed that a key to effective teaching in early childhood is the professional development of teachers, a process that can span formal educational experiences between high school and graduate school and include formal and informal training and mentoring experiences. Although the content of early childhood education professional development varies from state to state, across time professional development within each state became organized into professional development systems—sets of requirements and procedures by which states determine who is qualified to teach, together with the mechanisms states adopt for preparing and qualifying teachers. Because the regulation of teachers is a state responsibility and because there is less consensus around teacher qualifications in early childhood education, as opposed to the K–12 educational system, teacher qualifications and certification vary greatly among states. Thus, although every state has an early childhood education professional development system, the content of the system and its location in a particular agency within a state are extremely variable across the country. To add to this variability, many states have recently implemented quality rating systems to try to streamline what constitutes quality in early childhood education. These systems, tied or not to continuous improvement via a quality rating improvement system, are program standards in the form of rating scales that define the optimal and threshold conditions for caring for and preparing children for school and, in the case of quality rating improvement systems, for encouraging and rewarding program improvement. In theory, the goal of a quality rating system is to provide accountability to stakeholders that early childhood education programs in fact promote or enhance the learning and development of young children. Across states, there is variation between teacher qualifications in quality rating systems and those in professional development systems. Thus, the chief goal of this book is to examine and explore the degree of integration of state professional development systems and quality rating systems.

Along with the continuing development of quality rating systems are states' efforts to establish early childhood education competencies—statements that define what teachers need to know and do in order to create optimal learning opportunities for children. There is a clear theoretical link between these competencies and professional development systems. In the ideal world, the curriculum or content of professional development in a state would match the early childhood education competencies of the state. However, as with quality rating systems, early childhood education competencies have largely been developed and implemented outside of the state professional development systems. Furthermore, the early childhood education professional development system's domain is different from that of the K–12 professional development system. The domain of professional development for K–12 teachers and for many, but not all, early childhood education teachers is the state's higher education system, although training and education of early childhood education teachers can and does occur in alternative systems (e.g., child care resource and referral agencies and health and human services job training agencies). Thus, the second goal of this book is to examine and explore the degree of integration of state professional development systems and early childhood education competencies within and across states.

In 2008, the National Center for Research in Early Childhood Education (NCRECE) produced a white paper arguing that professional development systems should be better integrated with both quality rating systems and early childhood education competencies in order to improve the delivery of early childhood education services. (See the appendix for a copy of this document.) It was the intention of that paper to stimulate conceptualization and planning of the required research on the components of, and linkages among, the three types of systems, with an eye toward arriving at an evidence-driven system through which policy and program development would improve the quality of early childhood services offered to young children. The current book is a next step in this process.

The book is divided into two sections. In the first, leaders in the early childhood education policy field were invited to provide overviews of the three systems and explore their integration. In the first chapter of the section, Martha Zaslow and her coauthors tackle the complex reality of defining and measuring professional development. Early childhood professionals work in a variety of services, including family and center-based child care, Head Start, and preschool and prekindergarten programs. The authors argue that achieving agreement on common definitions and uniform measurement criteria for what is required of teachers and providers in these various sectors is an essential first step in integrating professional development into quality rating systems and early childhood education competencies and for ensuring effective teachers.

Lori Connors-Tadros and Barbara Coccodrilli Carlson continue and expand this argument for consensus across sectors in the second chapter, which is devoted primarily to the intersection and integration of quality rating and professional development systems. In this chapter, the authors propose a framework for a common language across these systems in order to align the regulation of programs, the financing of quality improvement, and accountability: Do quality rating systems work together with professional development systems to increase the quality of early childhood education services?

The third chapter in this section focuses on early childhood education competencies—what teachers should know in order to be effective in working with children. Sarah LeMoine and her coauthors examine the array of core knowledge requirements and competencies for early childhood teachers provided by disparate early childhood education sectors, including Head Start, Early Head Start, family and center-based child care, prekindergarten, kindergarten through third grade, early intervention, and special education. Continuing the theme of this first section of the book, the authors argue for a universal set of early childhood education competencies in order to achieve integration of the expectations, competencies, and requirements for early education professionals, regardless of their setting or stream of funding.

In the fourth and final chapter of this section, Pamela J. Winton and Tracey West ask how early childhood education competencies can guide professional development. The authors set forth a range of recommendations to address this question. Their premise is that national leadership and guidance must be provided to states to assist them in developing cross-sectoral early childhood professional development systems that align with national personnel standards, practice guidelines, competencies, and quality initiatives, such as accreditation, licensing, and quality rating improvement systems.

For the second section of this book, the leadership team of the NCRECE identified six states (Delaware, Kentucky, Maryland, New Mexico, Ohio, and Pennsylvania) that were, in their eyes, leaders in developing quality rating systems and early childhood education competencies and in the integration of professional development into these systems. The team then invited early childhood education and development doctoral students at the University of Virginia and University of California, Los Angeles, to participate in a project to examine systems and their integration within each state. The chapter authors completed detailed case studies for each state, using public web sites and interviews with key informants. Then they reviewed the case study material and identified overarching themes across the six case studies. These themes were expanded into the three chapters that make up Section II of this book.

Chapter 5 sets the stage for this analysis of systems and their integration. It includes a description of the quality rating systems, early childhood education competencies, and professional development systems in each of the selected states and then compares and contrasts qualifications that are required at each quality rating system level for various staff members. The chapter then goes on to examine, in turn, the structure, content, and delivery of professional development; quality rating system infrastructure support for professional development systems; and the incentives that have been found to facilitate staff participation in professional development. This chapter and its accompanying charts provide details on the systems in each of the selected states.

Chapter 6 explores how the actions of state agencies with regard to the professional development of the state's early childhood work force can help or hinder integration between quality rating systems and professional development systems. This chapter identifies the types of state agencies through which professional development policies are implemented and the bearing that the particular agency in which the system is located has on the types of professional development opportunities offered. Next, the ways in which states direct financial resources for professional development are discussed. Finally, the influence of state quality rating systems on the professional development of the early childhood work force is explored.

Chapter 7 begins the process of examining the evaluation of the integration of systems toward the larger goal of creating effective teachers through a professional development system. This chapter uses material from case studies to illustrate the elements of such an evaluation and discusses the process of within-state evaluations.

These state-based systems and their integration are part of a larger effort to provide good early childhood education to our youngest citizens. They are based on the assumption that if we are confident about what teachers need to know and be able to do to be successful in classrooms (i.e., if teachers possess well-defined early childhood education competencies), then we can build resources to prepare and support that knowledge and those skills and to certify teachers' competence (through professional development systems). We can then put in place accountability mechanisms that give teachers incentives to progress toward higher levels of competence and convey information about competence to stakeholders (via quality rating systems).

I

National-Level Concerns

1

Early Childhood Professional Development Definitions and Measurement Approaches

Martha Zaslow, Tamara Halle,
Kathryn Tout, and Debra Weinstein

The field of early childhood is currently receiving recognition and encouragement for its work toward the development of integrated early childhood systems. A growing number of states are working not just to improve components of the professional development they provide for the early childhood workforce, but to develop professional development systems that cut across sectors and serve all early childhood professionals (LeMoine, 2005, 2008). Nineteen states have put in place quality ratings and improvement systems, all specifying levels of professional development required for different quality ratings.

The early childhood field is also seeing explicit encouragement to link professional development systems and quality rating and improvement

Much of the work reported in this chapter concerning defining and measuring early childhood professional development was completed under Contract #HHSP233200500198U with the Administration for Children and Families, U.S. Department of Health and Human Services. The views presented in the chapter are those of the authors and do not represent the views of the Administration for Children and Families, U.S. Department of Health and systems into overarching early childhood systems. Such encouragement is apparent, for example, in the Obama administration's Early Learning Challenge Fund initiative (U.S. Department of Education, 2009). This initiative has not been yet been funded; however, the description of the initiative by the U.S. Department of Education makes clear a vision of systems integration that includes professional development and quality improvement among multiple components. The goal of the Early Learning Challenge Fund is to work toward uniform standards of quality across the various types of early care and education (child care, Head Start, and prekindergarten), including providing support for improvements in quality and ensuring that more children enter kindergarten ready for success in school. The U.S. Department of Education statement mentions the following components in early care and education systems: early learning standards, an evidence-based quality rating and improvement system (QRIS), program monitoring and improvement, a system of professional development, strategies for families to better assess quality in early childhood programs, screening and referrals of children, coordinated data systems for the age range from birth to 5 years, and developmentally appropriate curricula and assessment systems. Professional development is woven through this vision in multiple places, with explicit reference to comprehensive professional development systems.

This chapter argues that common definitions and measurement approaches to key aspects of early childhood professional development, referred to here as *professional development constructs*, are a foundation for integrated early childhood systems. Agreement among key stakeholders on definitions and measurement approaches to these constructs is central in codeveloping the elements of a professional development system, a QRIS, and an overarching system that includes both of these. Fundamental differences in how professional development constructs are measured in different systems or in components within a system (e.g., in requirements for professional development in Head Start, prekindergarten, and child care programs) can mean that aligning requirements

Human Services. The authors thank Richard Brandon, Donna Bryant, Carol Brunson Day, Cathie Field, Marilou Hyson, Lee Kreader, Valerie Krajec, Ivelisse Martinez-Beck, Sarah LeMoine, Kelly Maxwell, Dawn Ramsburg, Mousumi Sarkar, Linda Smith, Kathy Thornburg, Karen Tvedt, Jere Wallden, and Bobbie Weber of the Working Group on Defining and Measuring Early Childhood Professional Development for their numerous contributions toward recommendations for stronger and more consistent definitions and measures of professional development, many of which are summarized in this chapter. The authors also thank Ivelisse Martinez-Beck for her identification of the importance of this set of issues, not only for research, but also for policy and practice, as well as for her encouragement in working together toward, and sharing, common definition and measurement approaches. Finally, the authors thank Sarah LeMoine, Davida McDonald, and Alison Lutton for their insightful and extremely helpful suggestions on an earlier draft of this chapter.

across types of care for an integrated system is difficult or impossible (LeMoine, 2008). Further, the problem of lack of agreement in the definition and measurement of early childhood professional development within a state working toward an integrated system is compounded in any efforts that cut across states.

The chapter begins by summarizing areas in which problems with the definition and measurement of key early childhood professional development constructs have been identified. We note potential solutions to these issues based on the work of the members of the Working Group on Defining and Measuring Early Childhood Professional Development, convened by the Child Care Bureau, U.S. Department of Health and Human Services, in March 2004. We conclude by noting emerging issues in early childhood professional development research that suggest areas in which further work to reach agreement on definition and measurement will be warranted.

ISSUES IN THE DEFINITION AND MEASUREMENT OF CORE CONSTRUCTS IN EARLY CHILDHOOD PROFESSIONAL DEVELOPMENT

The absence of common definitions and measurement for key early childhood professional development constructs was first identified as a stumbling block for aggregating research findings at a meeting sponsored by the Science and Ecology of Early Development, or SEED, Consortium, a consortium of federal agencies, in February 2003. In preparation for the meeting, which focused on early childhood professional development as a contributor to children's school readiness, Kelly Maxwell, Cathie Feild, and Richard Clifford (2003, 2006) were asked to review the research and, where these were found to be lacking, propose common definitional and measurement approaches. To their surprise, the review of how key constructs were defined and measured revealed wide discrepancies that posed serious difficulty in seeking to determine, across research studies, whether specific elements of professional development mattered for the quality of early childhood settings or for child outcomes.

Although the discrepancies in definitional and measurement approaches can limit the degree to which research informs policy investments, the consortium was also concerned that they might also be an impediment in assessing the size and characteristics of the early childhood workforce nationally, in state work aimed at integrating professional development efforts across types of care, or in beginning work toward achieving QRISs. A subsequent meeting held in Washington, D.C., in February 2004 and sponsored by the Child Care Bureau and the Office of the Assistant Secretary for Planning and Evaluation of the U.S. Department of Health and Human Services brought together participants from early care and education agencies, members of state and national practice organizations, and researchers. There was clear confirmation that a lack of agreement on definitions and measurement permeated policy and practice efforts as well.

Following this meeting, the Working Group on Defining and Measuring Early Childhood Professional Development was formed to make progress in working toward common definitions and measures for professional development constructs and their use in policy and practice initiatives within and across states. (The group's statement of purpose, papers, and presentations may be seen on the Child Care and Early Education Research Connections web site, Collaborative Projects portal, Professional Development Definitions and Measures section, at http://www.childcareresearch.org.) Whereas Maxwell and colleagues' (2003) initial account of the existence of problems with definitional and measurement approaches drew upon the measures used to describe professional development in major studies of early childhood development, the February 2004 meeting confirmed that similar issues were appearing in state policy and practice efforts and in national efforts as well. In the next section, we distinguish between definitional and measurement issues, summarizing problems with each.

Definitional Issues

Maxwell and colleagues (2003) identified three core constructs pertaining to early childhood professional development: training, education, and credentialing. The key definitional issue relating to these constructs was a lack of clear distinctions among them—especially between education and training. Other definitional issues pertain to components within these constructs, especially credentialing, whose components also exhibited a lack of clear distinctions.

Maxwell and colleagues (2006) noted that in some research, the term *training* connotes all forms of professional development (e.g., classes contributing to higher education degrees, workshops that fulfill in-service licensing requirements but that do not contribute to higher education degrees, on-site technical assistance, participation in professional meetings); in other research, *training* refers only to classes or workshops; and in still other research, the term denotes only workshops that do not contribute to a higher education degree. This blurring of definitions has implications for policy makers in that the resources needed for extending the system of higher education are very different from the resources needed for extending the system of training that does not contribute toward higher education degrees. Policy makers are concerned with allocating resources effectively, and, toward that end, they seek information that is specific enough to help them target funding.

Maxwell and colleagues recommended defining *training* as "professional development activities that occur outside the formal education system. Training activities do not lead to a degree" (2006, p. 23) and defining *education* as "professional development activities that occur within a formal education system" (p. 23). (We follow their recommendation in the remainder of the chapter.) They noted that the mere location of a workshop or course cannot be its defining feature, as college courses are sometimes offered in early childhood program settings, and non–credit-bearing workshops can occur on college campuses. Participants in the February 2004 meeting concurred that being able to summarize the research separately on professional development that does and does not contribute to a higher education degree is critical to informing policy makers about how to target limited resources. Unfortunately, even very recent research does not make the sharp distinction between education and training proposed by Maxwell and colleagues, limiting the application of such research for policy and practice. (See, e.g., the definition of *training* in the meta-analysis by Fukkink & Lont, 2007.)

As regards the aforementioned lack of clear distinctions among the components of the broad construct of credentialing, Maxwell and colleagues recommended using the term *credential* as an umbrella construct encompassing, among other things, professional development that "convey[s] a certain status to the holders and provide[s] some assurance to consumers that the holders are qualified to provide designated services" (2006, p. 34). However, they noted confusion in regard to how to distinguish clearly among the key components of credentialing, such as licensing, certification, and the attainment of named credentials such as the Child Development Associate (CDA) credential. There is a need for clear distinctions among these components on the basis of whether the credential is for entry-level or more advanced work in early childhood, content, and auspices.

Licensing involves completing *minimal initial requirements* and then *ongoing requirements* for work in specific early childhood settings (e.g., child care centers) and is granted by state agencies such as departments of health and human services. Although training, as defined earlier, is generally accessible to all those in the early childhood workforce, licensing may require specific amounts and types of training in order to attain (preservice) and maintain (in-service) the license. A level of educational attainment and/or specific credentials may also be required for licensing. Ongoing updates of licensing requirements by the National Child Care Information Center (2007) indicate that whereas most states have in-service requirements for ongoing training for early childhood center teachers, only a minority have preservice requirements for teachers.

In contrast, certificates and specific credentials involve completing professional development (which may involve either education or training) *with particular content in order to achieve professional recognition for expertise.* Maxwell and colleagues (2006) reported that the CDA credential, a national credential in existence for more than 25 years, is the credential most widely reported in research. Moreover, when state licensing requirements call for a specific credential, the CDA is the most frequently noted as well, and there is a long history in Head Start of recognizing the CDA among its professional development requirements.

Although specific credentials are often sponsored by professional organizations or associations, certificates are frequently granted by state agencies, such as departments of education. Earning such certificates may involve taking a step beyond required levels of education in order to qualify to work with children of different age ranges or children with particular needs. For example, particular certificates may be required for work in prekindergarten or early elementary grades in public schools.

An important issue that arises in examining the research on credentials is the wide variation across states in requirements for licensing, specific credentials, and certificates (although it is helpful here that the CDA is a national program). Maxwell and colleagues (2006) noted that it is important for research not just to introduce the name of the credential when describing correlates in terms of quality or child outcomes, but to be very clear about the requirements and how long a credential remains current. It is inappropriate to reach broad conclusions about whether credentials do and do not matter when research across states may encompass a multitude of requirements. Any cross-state discussions about early childhood systems involving professional development will also need clear statements noting the requirements of state-specific credentials.

Measurement Issues

Even when there is agreement among researchers, policy makers, and practitioners on how the three core constructs of early childhood professional development are defined, lack of agreement on how they are measured can hinder efforts at alignment within and across systems. Further, gaps in measurement limit what can be gleaned from research and how a system accords recognition to differences in professional development.

Issues with measurement have been identified for each of the core constructs, and both Maxwell and colleagues and the Working Group on Defining and Measuring Early Childhood Professional Development (as summarized by Zaslow, Halle, McNamara, Weinstein, & Dent, 2007) have made recommendations for addressing them.

Education In order to align components of an early childhood system, levels of education need to be distinguished in the same way. Yet there are often important differences in the way distinctions are made among levels of educational attainment in both research and practice. For example, Maxwell and colleagues noted that in some systems for recording educational attainment, there is a single category of "some college" for those who have gone beyond high school without completing a bachelor's degree. Yet "if researchers hypothesize that teachers or providers with 3 years of college . . . provide different environments for children compared with teachers or providers who have taken only one college-level course, then it would be important to measure college education at a more detailed level" (Maxwell et al., 2006, p. 27). Also, some measurement approaches fold together "some college" and "associate's degree." Research by Thornburg (2006) provides evidence that making distinctions in the extent of lead teachers' education between high school and the completion of a bachelor's degree is indeed important in predicting observed quality in early childhood settings. Other research and state systems for documenting professional development fold together the completion of high school and the receipt of a GED. In aligning systems, it is important to determine which educational attainment distinctions are critical to make and then to make the same distinctions across the various types of early care and education.

Further issues arise in the measurement of coursework with content related to early childhood development. Maxwell and colleagues (2006) noted two general approaches to documenting such coursework: whether respondents have *any* related coursework and whether they have completed a *major* in early childhood development. However, there is wide variation in how surveys identify the content that is considered to be related to early childhood development (e.g., it may include courses in psychology or nursing), with some research simply leaving it to the respondent to note whatever coursework they perceive to be related.

Further, the label "degree in early childhood" can mask wide variation in the number and content of courses taken, whether they are intentionally sequenced, and whether they encompass the full period from birth to entry into school. In many instances, recognition is given to "related fields" as well as a major specifically in early childhood development. Russell (2004) questioned the utility of asking about a major in early childhood development and instead recommended asking for a listing of courses completed with content related to early development.

The National Registry Alliance (as summarized by Thornburg, 2006, and Wallden, 2005) suggested the importance of recording such courses prospectively rather than through retrospective recall. Both Thornburg and Wallden noted problems with recall at the level of specific courses completed. Their experience with verifying coursework also, unfortunately, suggests that some college coursework and degrees are reported for colleges that should not have been given recognition. States with early childhood professional development registries have the opportunity both to build into their systems a process for verifying specific courses as well as completed degrees and to develop consistent guidelines for what coursework can be considered related to early childhood development. A key issue for states that are planning to integrate registries into their systems is how to encourage participation so that registry information is available for most, if not all, members of the licensed workforce.

The measurement problems we have identified regarding levels of education for early childhood educators and caregivers may help to explain the recent finding that neither the completion of a bachelor's degree per se, nor the completion of such a degree with an early childhood major, among lead teachers in early childhood classrooms in the year prior to kindergarten is consistently related to better observed quality or gains in children's achievement (Early et al., 2007). Wide variation in the content of coursework for a bachelor's degree and for such a degree with an early childhood major may make it impossible to detect associations that would be found if there were clear criteria for what coursework should be considered relevant (Burchinal, Hyson, & Zaslow, 2008).

Training   Maxwell and colleagues (2006) noted multiple problems in respondents' reports of the extent of training they completed. Indeed, there is such wide variation in respondent recall of hours of training completed that researchers have questioned the validity of the data and have tended to collapse responses into the binary distinction of "any training" versus "no training."

Although recall of hours of training completed may be inaccurate, two further distinctions having to do with the extent of training have emerged from research as potentially useful and important: *recency* of training and whether the training was *intensive*. A key issue for those developing integrated early childhood systems is whether to establish a criterion in terms of the time frame within which training has been completed. A review by Tout, Zaslow, and Berry (2006) summarized evidence that recent or ongoing training may be more likely than earlier training to affect practice. A review of available survey instruments completed as part of the Working Group efforts identified "training completed in the past 12 months" as the most frequently used marker for recently completed training (Zaslow et al., 2007). The ongoing documentation of training by registries makes information on recency readily available.

The Working Group on Defining and Measuring Early Childhood Professional Development recommended that a distinction be made between single, stand-alone workshops and more intensive training involving a planned sequence of sessions. The Midwest Child Care Research Consortium (Raikes et al., 2006) found that in a sample of child care settings in four Midwestern states, observed quality was related to intensive training, defined as training in a particular approach to working with young children (such as the WestEd Training Program for Infant and Toddler Caregivers), or a curricular approach (such as High/Scope or Creative Curriculum), across all three types of care considered (infant/toddler center-based care, preschool center-based care, and family child care). This distinction between single-session workshops and training involving a planned sequence was incorporated into the survey conducted by the National Association of Child Care Resource and Referral Agencies (NACCRRA) of the training provided by child care resource and referral agencies (Smith et al., 2006).

Just as there is a lack of clear guidance for documenting what higher education coursework is clearly related to early childhood development, there is a lack of guidance in identifying the content of training around which it is important to build systems. NACCRRA has identified this deficiency as an extremely important issue, noting that training requirements for licensing that are articulated simply in terms of the number of preservice and in-service training hours are resulting in some early childhood caregivers and educators repeating the same training each year and therefore never receiving preparation in key content areas (Sarkar, 2006; Smith, 2006).

Maxwell and colleagues (2006) noted that researchers have often collected, but then not used, information on the content of training, suggesting that there are issues of how best to collapse the extensive number of categories on which respondents report. In her work as part of the Working Group on Defining and Measuring Early Childhood Professional Development, Hyson and Biggar (2006) proposed that the National Association for the Education of Young Children (NAEYC) standards for professional preparation (see summary in Hyson & Biggar, 2006) could serve as a starting point for identifying a limited and clear set of content areas to describe training. This recommendation was then incorporated into pilot work by the National Registry Alliance on the implementation of a common core of measures of professional development across selected state early childhood professional development registries (National Registry Alliance, 2006; Wallden, 2005). The Alliance recommends ongoing and current recording of training completed, rather than retrospective reporting. As with the completion of college coursework, this approach permits confirmation that the training completed was offered by a qualified trainer (if the state has a trainer approval process) under the auspices of an agency or organization recognized by the state. In addition, the recommendation permits verification of participation in such training. At present, approval of training often differs by sector (e.g., training required and approved for a child care provider may differ from that required and approved for a prekindergarten teacher). A goal for integrated professional development systems is to align the training that is offered and approved across sectors of early care and education.

Following their participation in the Working Group on Defining and Measuring Early Childhood Professional Development, NACCRRA leadership moved toward recommending that states require that preservice and in-service training cover specific content areas, using a "distribution requirement" approach. NACCRRA has structured, and is now piloting, a new software system to identify and record training in specific content areas.

Credentials A key foundation for professional development systems and QRISs will be a common measurement approach to credentials. Head Start, prekindergarten and child care, and other programs require different credentials that are impossible to align and calibrate across types of early care and education. These different requirements will serve as barriers to collaboration across types of programs (such as collaboration between prekindergarten and child care programs) or to the sharing of professional development opportunities. This issue is being addressed in states that are working to develop comprehensive early childhood professional development systems (LeMoine, 2008).

The preceding measurement issues pertain to aligning credentials for providers and programs. There are also measurement issues regarding how credentials are understood by consumers. It is important not to make assumptions about what consumers understand, but to provide information about the requirements for all types of credentials, as well as information about providers and programs that are exempt from particular requirements.

Those who develop professional development systems, QRISs, and overarching integrated systems will need to determine which certificates and credentials to recognize as part of their systems. Finally, the Working Group recommended distinguishing between fulfilling the credits required for a CDA credential through college coursework or through training and confirming not only that a credential had ever been completed, but that it is current.

Looking Across as Well as Within States

Although we have emphasized the importance within states of having clear definitions and measures of professional development that can be aligned across types of early care and education, definition and measurement are also important in efforts that cut across states. A first key consideration is that families may move across states, so confusion regarding the differences in definitions of professional development across states can limit the extent to which families make informed decisions.

A recent NACCRRA report regarding families in the military illustrates this issue (Smith & Sarkar, 2008). Especially as they move across state lines and face different state requirements and terminology, military families often make incorrect assumptions about the licensing status of the care they are considering, and the correctness of their assumptions is critical to the receipt of assistance in paying for care within the military:

> Parents' confusion over their child care provider's licensing status is not surprising, as most states use terms such as certification, registration, licensing and exempt-care to define the different degrees of licensing status for providers, and often these terminologies have different meanings across state lines. For example, Arizona allows [family child care] providers to voluntarily register themselves in a state-maintained database if they are caring for fewer than six children. These providers are called "registered" providers, but they are neither inspected by the state or local government nor are they required to adhere to any standards regarding health and safety set by the state. Arizona also has "certified" providers, who care for six or more children. These providers are required to meet state standards, and are inspected by the state. In most states, these providers would be called "licensed" providers, but in Arizona they are called "certified providers." So it is not surprising that a military family moving from Arizona to Delaware would think that a certified provider would meet the military's requirements to provide fee assistance. (p. 21)

The need to transfer information across state lines may confront providers as well as consumers. Providers who move to a new state may face difficulties transferring information on their professional development to a state that uses different terminology or makes different distinctions in regard to level and content of education or training. In an effort to address this issue, The National Registry Alliance is piloting the use of a common set of definitions and providing guidance on the use of parallel measurement approaches across states (Wallden, 2005).

Another key area that cuts across states and in which common definitions and measurement would be extremely useful is the need to measure the size and characteristics of the early childhood workforce. Brandon and Martinez-Beck (2006) noted that there are multiple reasons for policy makers to need reliable national estimates of the size and characteristics of the early childhood workforce, including providing a basis for estimating what financing would be required for alternative approaches to improving quality and carrying out economic impact analyses of the contributions of the early childhood sector to the economy. Yet definitional issues impede national data collection efforts. The definitional issues here pertain both to who is included as a member of the early childhood workforce and to how characteristics of that workforce are measured.

Regarding who is encompassed in national data collection efforts, Brandon and Martinez-Beck (2006) noted that data collection by the Bureau of Labor Statistics includes two related categories: child care worker and preschool teacher. The child care worker category is defined in a way that does not encompass either the proprietors of licensed family child care homes or unlicensed family, friend, and neighbor caregivers. The preschool teacher category focuses on teachers in school-based programs, thereby excluding early educators in Head Start programs and other center-based programs not located in school settings.

Census Bureau data collection does include family child care providers. However, Brandon and Martinez-Beck (2006) noted that preschool and kindergarten teachers are combined into a single category and the data collection approach could miss center-based providers of younger children. Family, friend, and neighbor caregivers also are excluded.

Separate administrative data collection systems exist for child care subsidies, Head Start, and early childhood programs under the auspices of state departments of education. This is problematic in that individuals may be in early childhood settings that receive funding from more than one source. In addition, these administrative data collection systems do not encompass members of the workforce who are not in early childhood settings that receive funding from any of these public sources.

Brandon and Martinez-Beck (2006) noted the potential for national estimates, at least of licensed members of the early childhood workforce, through aggregating across state data collection for market rate surveys. However, definition and measurement issues would be critical: "If states were to adopt appropriate sampling methods; consistent definitions of [early childhood education] occupations, qualifications, and settings; and consistent timeframes, then such data could form the basis of a national [early childhood education] workforce data system" (p. 72). They urged the consideration of a model like that developed by the National Center for Education Statistics of the U.S. Department of Education for using common definitions in the collection of data regarding staff in schools across the 50 states.

PROGRESS AND RESOURCES

A set of resources available from members of the Working Group on Defining and Measuring Early Childhood Professional Development may be of use in deciding upon definitions and measures to use in state early childhood systems:

- A review of national and state surveys was conducted to identify the items in national and state surveys that best address the definitional and measurement issues summarized in the preceding section. On the basis of this review, a white paper was developed with a set of recommended survey measures based on publicly available data collection instruments (Zaslow et al., 2007). The recommended set of measures may help to provide a foundation for the elements of state early childhood systems concerning professional development.

- The National Registry Alliance is conducting pilot work toward implementing a common core of measures of early childhood professional development in selected states. A document on the organization's web site (National Registry Alliance, 2006) provides guidance on how to develop measures that are appropriate for specific state early childhood professional development registries and that reflect a common set of definitions and measurement recommendations. Such guidance helps to anticipate the need to recognize professional development on an ongoing basis and in a similar way across types of early care and education within states. At the same time, it recognizes the need for early educators or caregivers to transfer information about their professional development if they move across states.

- NACCRRA's work on content area requirements for training and how those requirements are recorded in the organization's software is of potential use for those developing state early childhood systems. In addition, NACCRRA's (2008) work on the qualification of trainers and those providing technical assistance may be useful to those states which are interested in introducing information about the qualifications of those providing professional development into their early childhood systems.

- Presentations by Weber (e.g., 2005) as part of the Working Group on Defining and Measuring Early Childhood Professional Development underscore the potential importance of developing a common identifier for members of the early childhood workforce to be used across state data systems so that information on their professional development can be made available and used consistently across elements of an integrated state early childhood system. Weber discussed ways to link data to minimize the need to collect information multiple times for different data systems and to ensure data quality. At the same time, she pointed out the priority that needs to be placed on data security and confidentiality.

- NAEYC's Early Childhood Workforce Systems Initiative (LeMoine, 2008) provides a guide for policy makers to work toward an integrated professional development system. The report recommends that state policies require the collection of specific data on professional development, as well as the alignment, sharing, and nonduplication of data across sectors. In addition, the report recommends policies that include specific requirements for disaggregated data by type of setting, demographics, and primary financing source(s). NAEYC also developed an online database of existing policies in each of the areas outlined by the report (http://www.naeyc.org/policy/ecwsi#database).

EMERGING ISSUES

Recent research on early childhood professional development suggests that it may be meaningful to document characteristics of professional development beyond those typically collected at present. Extending the range of professional development characteristics would present new challenges in terms of definitions and measurement. In this concluding section, we summarize research on three issues pointing to the potential importance of extending the professional development constructs on which those in the early childhood field regularly collect data.

Markers of the Quality of Professional Development

We have noted that contrary to expectations, recent research has found no consistent association between the attainment of a bachelor's degree per se or a bachelor's degree involving a major related to early childhood development with the quality of early childhood classrooms or children's achievement gains during the year prior to kindergarten (Early et al., 2007). Although the wide range in the number and content of courses required for a bachelor's degree is one possible basis for this unexpected pattern of findings, another possibility encompasses, but goes beyond, the number and nature of courses completed. According to Hyson, Tomlinson, and Morris (2009), research has not

> examined quality, and quality-improvement efforts, in teacher education programs. It is unlikely that a degree from a low-quality program would result in excellent or perhaps even adequate teaching and, therefore, in significant benefits for children. For this reason, a productive

next step may be to examine the extent to which high quality may or may not be present in early childhood teacher education programs and what factors may facilitate or impede efforts by these programs to raise their quality.

Hyson and colleagues (2009) noted that of approximately 450 higher education programs granting bachelor's degrees and graduate degrees in early childhood, only about half are accredited according to NAEYC standards under the auspices of the National Council for the Accreditation of Teacher Education (NCATE). Further, approximately 25% of initial applications for accreditation are not successful. Hyson and colleagues noted that unsuccessful applications can reflect the way in which materials are prepared for consideration and not just the quality of the program. However, a review found recurring program-related issues in rejected applications, including field placements that were not of high quality or that lacked supervision, student assignments and assessments not considered to be in keeping with the NAEYC standards, and faculty without appropriate background in early childhood.

A survey of 250 directors of higher education programs in early childhood identified both priorities for strengthening programs and challenges the directors felt that the programs were facing. Among the priorities for strengthening their programs, respondents identified strengthening student skills in implementing curricula, in carrying out child assessments, and in working with families. However, directors rarely noted as a priority strengthening teacher interactions with individual children or improving student ability to access and use research. When asked what they most needed to assist them in their efforts to strengthen their programs, directors indicated the need for more faculty, more time for instruction, and more institutional support for their programs. When asked what they were currently doing to strengthen their programs, directors noted that they were working to strengthen assessments of students, field placements, and courses. Yet most directors indicated a lack of budgetary or institutional support for increasing faculty capacity.

These findings raise the possibility that researchers should be measuring not only the completion of a higher education degree in early childhood education, but also the quality of the degree-granting program. Yet not all institutions of higher education participate in the NCATE–NAEYC process. In addition, as Hyson and colleagues noted, there is not yet a body of research involving direct observations of the graduates of accredited versus unaccredited degree programs examining differences in their practices within the classroom. Such research should encompass not only whether the degree-granting program was accredited, but also the extent to which the early childhood professional goes on to participate in a setting in which there is ongoing support and supervision (discussed further shortly). It may be that the combination of the quality of the education program and the quality of the work environment together predict practice, rather than either one alone. (We note that NAEYC has also been developing an associate's degree accreditation process.)

Using the accreditation of degree-granting programs as a marker of quality would fail to provide a marker of quality for the professional development completed by those without a higher education degree. As we have noted, states are beginning to include markers of the quality of training (including approval of trainers) in their data systems and NACCRRA is identifying best practices for both training and technical assistance. Just as research is needed regarding whether accredited higher education programs have graduates with classroom practices that are observably stronger, it will also be important to ask directly whether it is possible to observe stronger caregiving practices (or greater improvement in caregiving practice) when members of the early childhood workforce participate in training by certified trainers and pursue training focused on a range of recommended content. As with education, such research will need to take into account supports and supervision in the current work environment as well as quality of training.

The early childhood field is at an early stage in understanding the usefulness of collecting data on the quality of training or higher education programs. However, this is an emerging issue that states may want to monitor. Evidence may confirm that including markers of professional development quality is of importance, and the inclusion of such markers in state data collection may create pressure on providers of both training and higher education degree programs to monitor and invest in the quality of their programs.

Markers of Participation in Individualized Practice-Focused Professional Development

A further issue for states to consider in working toward common definitions and measures of early childhood professional development is whether, and if so, how, to capture participation in individualized practice-focused professional development. Recent research on professional development and on the implementation of curricula in early childhood settings has focused on approaches that involve working individually with early educators or caregivers, often at their places of work, on the direct implementation of positive practices. Implementing these practices often involves utilizing approaches such as the modeling of interactions with children, observation and the provision of feedback on the early educator or caregiver's practice in the classroom or group, and reflection and discussion.

Just as one indication of how widespread the use of individualized practice-focused approaches has become, of 18 projects funded by the U.S. Department of Education in 2003, 2004, and 2005 to strengthen professional development for early educators working in low-income communities across the country, some form of individualized practice-focused approach to professional development was nearly universal, with professional development almost always combining on-site work with a mentor or coach with knowledge-focused coursework or training (Tout, Halle, Zaslow, & Starr, 2009).

A recent review of the research on early childhood professional development underscores the fact that many, *but not all*, of the individualized practice-focused approaches to professional development have shown evidence of positive effects on practice in working with children or on child outcomes (Zaslow, Tout, Halle, Whittaker, & Lavelle, 2010). Indeed, Tout and colleagues (2010) have underscored the importance of going beyond broad descriptions of such approaches to identifying in greater detail the specific ways in which professional development is carried out within those approaches. For example, goals for individualized practice-focused approaches may be set by the educator or by the coach, mentor, or technical assistance provider. Also, there may or may not be tight linkages with the content of coursework or training, such that each session of individualized work may focus on content just introduced through such knowledge-focused components, or there may be no explicit link between the content and timing of knowledge- and practice-focused components. Describing the specific features of practice-focused professional development will be critical to distinguishing between approaches that are and are not effective in improving practice and child outcomes.

There is enough promising evidence to suggest the need to build toward identification of the important elements of practice-focused professional development for states to monitor and track and to work toward agreed-upon definitions and measures of these elements. It is noteworthy that NACCRRA convened a working group to develop common data elements, focusing on the provision and receipt of technical assistance.

Markers of Context

A final issue for states to consider as they work toward common definitions and measures of professional development to incorporate into their early childhood systems is how to reflect key features of the context within which an early educator or caregiver is working. Research by Vu, Jeon, and Howes (2008) indicates that states may need to go beyond the simple consideration of whether an early educator or caregiver has a bachelor's degree—a perspective of the educator or caregiver as operating solo—to a

perspective that also takes into account the resources and supports provided in the setting in which he or she is teaching. In their research focusing on early educators in California, having a bachelor's degree predicted
quality in settings in which there were fewer resources and supports, but
not in settings that had more resources and supports.

In further work, Fuligni, Howes, Lara-Cinisomo, and Karoly (2009)
presented evidence that early childhood settings have differing profiles in
terms of the combined level of education of caregivers, on the one hand,
and opportunities for their ongoing monitoring and support, on the other.
Four clusters emerged from their analyses: settings in which caregivers
had generally lower levels of education, but had ongoing monitoring and
support; settings in which caregivers had generally lower levels of education, but lacked ongoing monitoring and support; settings with better educated caregivers who had professional development background
specifically in early childhood; and settings with better educated caregivers
who did not have professional development background specifically in
early childhood. Family child care providers tended to have lower levels of
education and ongoing monitoring and support. Private child care centers
tended to have caregivers with a combination of low education and high
ongoing monitoring and support. Extending the earlier research by Vu
and colleagues (2008), which focused only on center-based care, this more
recent research found that having a bachelor's degree was associated with
more authoritative beliefs about children specifically in family child care,
the setting involving the least ongoing monitoring and support. Across
both studies, then, having a higher education degree may emerge as more
important in achieving quality among caregivers or educators who are
receiving less monitoring and support. Environments with more ongoing
monitoring and support may be providing a context that can be seen as
continuing professional development through oversight and support or as
compensating for less education.

These findings suggest that what is needed is documentation of ongoing monitoring and support as a facet of early childhood professional
development. Researchers have hypothesized that specific professional
development approaches may be more effective when program administrators and all teachers from a setting participate jointly in group training
or education (e.g., Dickinson & Brady, 2006). Administrators may provide
important signals about whether on-site practice-focused professional
development is endorsed and supported. Educators may provide mutual
reinforcement as they implement an approach learned through professional development.

Thus, an emerging issue is the importance of considering contextual
factors in the work settings of those pursuing professional development.
As the research on this set of issues moves forward, it will be important to

identify which features of early childhood settings are important to measure and how best to measure them. Research to date suggests that ongoing monitoring and support, and whether professional development was pursued by individuals or by cohorts from a particular early childhood setting, should be considered.

CONCLUSION

This chapter points to the importance of clarifying definitions of early childhood professional development and utilizing consistent measures that make key distinctions in terms of the extent, content, and quality of professional development for aligning different components of an overarching early childhood system. Recent work provides a sufficient basis to begin to address this challenge. However, it will be important to revisit this set of issues over time as new evidence on how best to understand the key facets of early childhood professional development emerges.

STUDY QUESTIONS

1. What are the three core constructs of early childhood professional development?

2. In addition to recall of hours of training completed, what two further distinctions in terms of extent of training have emerged from research as potentially useful and important?

3. How does measurement of early childhood professional development differ from definition of professional development, and why is it also important?

REFERENCES

Brandon, R., & Martinez-Beck, I. (2006). Estimating the size and characteristics of the United States early care and education workforce. In M. Zaslow & I. Martinez-Beck (Eds.), *Critical issues in early childhood professional development* (pp. 49–76). Baltimore: Paul H. Brookes Publishing Co.

Burchinal, M., Hyson, M., & Zaslow, M. (2008). Competencies and credentials for early childhood educators: What do we know and what do we need to know? *National Head Start Dialog Briefing Paper* (Vol. 11, No. 1).

Dickinson, D.K., & Brady, J.P. (2006). Toward effective support for language and literacy through professional development. In M. Zaslow & I. Martinez-Beck (Eds.), *Critical issues in early childhood professional development* (pp. 141–170). Baltimore: Paul H. Brookes Publishing Co.

Early, D.M., Maxwell, K.L., Burchinal, M., Alva, S., Bender, R.H., Cai, et al. (2007). Teachers' education, classroom quality, and young children's academic skills: Results from seven studies of preschool programs. *Child Development, 78,* 558–580.

Fukkink, R.G., & Lont, A. (2007). Does training matter? A meta-analysis and review of caregiver training studies. *Early Childhood Research Quarterly, 22,* 294–311.

Fuligni, A.S., Howes, C., Lara-Cinisomo, S., & Karoly, L. (2009). Diverse pathways in early childhood professional development: An exploration of early educators in public preschools, private preschools and family child care homes. *Early Education and Development, 20,* 507–526.

Hyson, M., & Biggar, H. (2006). NAEYC's standards for early childhood professional preparation: Getting from here to there. In M. Zaslow & I. Martinez-Beck (Eds.), *Critical issues in early childhood professional development* (pp. 283–308). Baltimore: Paul H. Brookes Publishing Co.

Hyson, M., Tomlinson, H., & Morris, C. (2009). Quality improvement in early childhood teacher education: Faculty perspectives and recommendations for the future. *Early Childhood Research and Practice, 11*(1).

LeMoine, S. (2005, December). *State professional development systems.* Symposium on Defining and Measuring Early Childhood Professional Development: Update and Request for Input, Meetings of the National Association for the Education of Young Children, Washington, DC.

LeMoine, S. (2008). *Workforce designs: A policy blueprint for state early childhood professional development systems.* Washington, DC: National Association for the Education of Young Children. Retrieved April 6, 2010, from http://www.naeyc.org/files/naeyc/file/policy/ecwsi/Workforce_Designs.pdf

Maxwell, K.L., Feild, C.C., & Clifford, R.M. (2003, February). *Defining and measuring professional development.* Paper presented at the Meeting on Early Childhood Professional Development and Training and Children's Successful Transition to Elementary School, sponsored by the Science and Ecology of Early Development (SEED) consortium of federal agencies with research focusing on early childhood development, Washington, DC.

Maxwell, K.L., Feild, C.C., & Clifford, R.M. (2006). Toward better definition and measurement of early childhood professional development. In M. Zaslow & I. Martinez-Beck (Eds.), *Critical issues in early childhood professional development* (pp. 21–48). Baltimore: Paul H. Brookes Publishing Co.

National Association of Child Care Resource and Referral Agencies. (2008, June). *NACCRRA Quality Assurance CCR & R Provider Services Best Practices.* Retrieved August 7, 2009, from http://www.naccrra.org/programs/qap/docs/Best_Practices_Provider_June08.pdf

National Child Care Information Center. (2007). *State requirements for minimum preservice qualifications and annual ongoing training hours for child care center teachers and master teachers in 2007* (updated April 2009). Retrieved April 6, 2010, from http://nccic.acf.hhs.gov/pubs/cclicensingreq/cclr-teachers.html

National Registry Alliance. (2006, January). *National Registry Alliance core data elements: Achieving consistency among member states.* Retrieved from http://www.registryalliance.org

Raikes, H.H., Torquati, J., Hegland, S., Raikes, H.A., Scott, J., Messner, L., et al. (2006). Studying the culture of quality early education and care: A cumulative approach to measuring characteristics of the workforce and relations to quality in four Midwestern states. In M. Zaslow & I. Martinez-Beck (Eds.), *Critical issues in early childhood professional development* (pp. 111–136). Baltimore: Paul H. Brookes Publishing Co.

Russell, S. (2004, September). *Discussant's comments prepared for the conference Creating a National Plan for the Education of 4-year-olds*. Washington DC: Brookings Institution.

Sarkar, M. (2006, February). *Community-based training: Developing national standards and a tracking system*. Symposium on Emerging Research on Caregiver Training, National Symposium of the National Association of Child Care Resource and Referral Agencies, Washington, DC.

Smith, L., & Sarkar, M. (2008, September). *Making child care quality possible: Lessons learned from NACCRRA's military partnerships*. Arlington, VA: National Association of Child Care Resource and Referral Agencies.

Smith, L.K., Sarkar, M., Perry-Manning, L., & Schmalzried, B. (2006, November). *NACCRRA's national survey of child care resource and referral training*. Arlington, VA: National Association of Child Care Resource and Referral Agencies. Retrieved April 6, 2010, from http://www.naccrra.org

Summary of themes from Workshop on Defining and Measuring Early Childhood Professional Development. (February, 2004). Retrieved April 6, 2010, from the Child Care and Early Education Research Connections web site, section on Collaborative Projects, Materials from Workgroup on Defining and Measuring Early Childhood Professional Development, http://www.researchconnections.org/files/meetings/pddm/themes.pdf

Thornburg, K. (2006, November). *Overview of research from the Midwest Child Care Research Consortium*. Paper presented at Symposium on Defining and Measuring Early Childhood Professional Development, Meetings of the National Association for the Education of Young Children, Atlanta, GA.

Tout, K., Halle, T., Zaslow, M., & Starr, R. (2009). *Evaluation of the Early Childhood Educator Professional Development Program*. Prepared for U.S. Department of Education, Office of Planning, Evaluation and Policy Development, Policy and Program Studies Service.

Tout, K., Zaslow, M., & Berry, D. (2006). Quality and qualifications: Links between professional development and quality in early care and education settings. In M. Zaslow & I. Martinez-Beck (Eds.), *Critical issues in early childhood professional development* (pp. 77–110). Baltimore: Paul H. Brookes Publishing Co.

U.S. Department of Education. (July 2009). *Early Learning Challenge Fund*. Retrieved August 7, 2009, from http://www.ed.gov/about/inits/ed/earlylearning/elcf-factsheet.html

Vu, J.A., Jeon, H., & Howes, C. (2008). Formal education, credential, or both: Early childhood program classroom practices. *Early Education and Development*, *19*(3), 479–504.

Wallden, J. (2005, December). *The work of the National Registry Alliance in working towards agreed upon definitions for early childhood professional development*. Paper presented at a symposium on Defining and Measuring Early Childhood Professional Development: Update and Request for Input, Meetings of the National Association for the Education of Young Children, Washington, DC.

Weber, R. (2005, December). *Describing the child care workforce at the state level*. Paper presented at a symposium on Defining and Measuring Early Childhood Professional Development: Update and Request for Input, Meetings of the National Association for the Education of Young Children, Washington, DC.

Zaslow, M., Halle, T., McNamara, M., Weinstein, D., & Dent, A. (2007, July). *Working towards a recommended common core of measures of early childhood professional development: Issues and preliminary recommendations.* Washington, DC: Child Trends. Retrieved April 6, 2010, from http://www.childcareresearch.org/childcare/resources/12685/pdf

Zaslow, M., Tout, K., Halle, T., Whittaker, J. & Lavelle, B. (2010). *Towards the identification of features of effective professional development for early childhood educators.* Prepared for Policy and Program Studies Service, Office of Planning, Evaluation and Policy Development, U.S. Department of Education.

2

Integrating Quality Rating Systems and Professional Development Systems in Early Childhood

Lori Connors-Tadros and Barbara Coccodrilli Carlson

Challenged by the fragmentation of the field, state[1] decision makers are increasingly investing in quality improvement systems to support a diverse group of early childhood and school-age programs and practitioners. A quality improvement system offers a sound option for addressing fragmentation by connecting requirements, incentives, and supports that help programs and practitioners improve quality over time. Quality rating systems (QRSs) and professional development systems, two key types of quality improvement systems, offer policy makers and state leaders the opportunity to align investments, policies, and practices in order to maximize resources and benefit greater numbers of programs and practitioners. The intention and hope of these systemic approaches to improving quality is that more, or even *all*, children, will have access to high-quality teaching to support learning and development.

---

[1]Throughout this chapter, we use the term *state* to be inclusive of states and territories.

PURPOSE OF THE CHAPTER

Policy makers face increasing pressure to expand the scope and scale of quality improvement systems to reach all programs, practitioners, and children, and to ensure significant outcomes and accountability for investments. This objective requires that policy makers and researchers pay serious attention to the status, as well as the degree of alignment and integration, of QRSs and professional development systems. This chapter begins with a short discussion of the research on quality—at the system, program, and individual level—to set the context for a discussion of the current realities concerning the two types of systems. The chapter identifies both the opportunities and the gaps in the integration and coordination of systemic quality improvement efforts, along the way suggesting outstanding questions and areas of further research. A proposed framework for a common language to define the cross-cutting components of systems is offered to help unite and strengthen the alignment across the subsystems of early childhood and school-age learning, with the goal of, ultimately, enhancing teacher effectiveness.

DEFINITIONS OF QUALITY AT THE MACRO AND MICRO LEVELS

QRSs and professional development systems emerged over the last decade as a policy response to the generally low level of quality found in child care. These systems and subsystems often operate independently or on parallel levels, and to date, research into how they overlap, coordinate, and align to reach all practitioners and influence teaching quality has been lacking. But certainly, it is necessary not only to consider how these systems, at the macro and micro levels, define quality, but also to examine the theories of change that undergird them, in order to understand how they could or do influence teaching practice.

Quality at the System Level

The key elements of QRSs and professional development systems have been defined in the field, although they are customized in different ways, depending on the goals of each state or community. QRSs generally focus on standards of program or practitioner practice, mechanisms to monitor quality and ensure accountability, strategies to engage and support programs and practitioners, financing for incentives and services, and communication strategies to inform parents and consumers (Mitchell, 2005; Satkowski, 2009). Professional development systems focus on the same elements (NCCIC, 2009; Lemoine, 2008).

QRSs and professional development systems have matured over the past decade, as new research on quality has increased the evidence base on the indicators that affect or predict quality. Consequently, states and localities are redefining and revising the definitions of each of their elements, focusing particularly on specific indicators of quality. In addition, as states gain experience in implementing these complex systems in an increasingly challenging political and fiscal environment, state leaders face new questions regarding how best to support the quality of early childhood and school-age care. In essence, states must dig deeper into the subsystems that undergird systemic approaches to quality improvement. Among these subsystems are the following:

- *Regulatory*. Licensing regulations are generally considered the floor of quality and are often the first gateway that programs face in entering systems of quality improvement. As states seek to strengthen the alignment between their regulatory and quality improvement systems in order to engage programs and practitioners from the wide array of care settings, inconsistencies in standards across settings often emerge. For example, in many states, school-based prekindergarten or school-age programs may be exempt from licensing, necessitating alternative strategies to support access to quality systems.

- *Accountability*. State leaders want information that helps them monitor the impact of investments in systems in order to improve quality for programs, practitioners, and children. Measures documenting and tracking quality are not always reliable or valid for the diversity of programs and practitioners served (Child Trends, 2009), and the costs of implementing data systems, including observational and other accountability strategies, can be significant.

- *Financing*. Quality improvement systems require a substantial up-front investment in infrastructure to support the alignment of their elements and the incentives to encourage access and ensure the persistence and improvement of programs and practitioners (Zellman & Perlman, 2008). In the current fiscal climate, state leaders are facing critical questions regarding the supports they are able to offer, how public and private funds are used, and how to expand quality improvement systems to ensure scalability and sustainability (Stoney, 2004).

Quality at the Program Level

Child care quality at the program level has focused on structural elements that typically are subject to regulation, such as group size; *practitioner characteristics*, such as motivation for providing care; and *process* elements of the setting experienced by children, such as caregiver–child interactions. These components of quality have been investigated in order to understand their links to program and child outcomes since policymakers want to know that children's experiences in all types of settings are supportive of learning and healthy development.

Such studies typically use global assessments of child care quality that are intended to measure both structural and process aspects of quality. Although most QRSs currently use environmental rating scales to measure quality (NCCIC, March 2010), many states now assess program quality in various settings and across a broader developmental age range with new tools and measures informed by a growing body of research. The measurement of quality at the program level is a significant issue for QRSs in particular, as policy makers are increasingly called on to ensure accountability and report quantifiable data to track progress and the results of investments (Tout, Zaslow, Halle, & Forry, 2009). However, key questions related to *who* determines program quality (i.e., are the findings determined by self-assessment or verified by outside raters?) and *how the information is used* (i.e., are findings used to determine ratings of quality or the award of incentives?) are vexing state leaders as they attempt to balance issues of access, cost, and accountability.

New research is also providing a more nuanced understanding of the factors that affect program quality particularly in professional development systems and QRSs. For example, research indicates 1) that both the content and format of professional development and training opportunities have important implications for improving the quality of specific types of programs; 2) that personal characteristics of staff, such as motivation and ability to engage children in positive relationships, influences outcomes of children; and 3) that administrative functions and leadership characteristics of program leaders affect the ability of practitioners to engage and sustain practices associated with quality (Weber & Trauten, 2008). On the basis of this emerging research, state leaders are attempting to revise and refine the policies, practices, and investments in quality improvement systems in order to realize greater and more sustainable gains in program quality. For example, many states are using new tools to measure teacher–child interaction in QRSs and professional development systems, and leaders are placing a greater emphasis on the use of coaches and mentors to support processes of change in programs and practitioners. Still, significant questions remain regarding what sustains program quality over time and how issues of culture and race, for example, can be effectively addressed in QRSs and professional development systems.

Quality at the Individual Level

QRSs and professional development systems have appealed to policy makers because they offer a logical framework for connecting and aligning policies at the state level with practices at the program level. The work becomes more complex for state leaders when they consider the broad diversity of the early childhood and school-age workforce at the individual level. The education and training of practitioners forms the touchstone— or key intersection point—for the ability of QRSs and professional development systems to realize their goals of quality improvement—for programs, practitioners, and, ultimately, children. However, despite ongoing new research, the field is still struggling with critical questions, such as the following:

- What level of qualifications and education is necessary for improving quality?

- What combination of education, training, and support has the greatest impact on individual practitioners' practices related to quality programming and thereby on outcomes for children and youth?

- What specific skills, training, and experience of practitioners serving specific age groups, such as infants and toddlers or school-age children and youth, support quality?

CURRENT NATIONAL LANDSCAPE OF QUALITY RATING SYSTEMS

Licensing is seen as not sufficient, or particularly malleable due to the state regulatory environment, as a systemic approach to improving quality. Therefore, *QRSs* have emerged and proliferated, nationwide. In large part, policy makers believe that QRSs, employing an easily recognizable symbol of quality, such as stars (similar to those used to rate restaurants) fuel consumer demand for quality care. A market approach to improving quality, in combination with a strengthening of the coordination among separate quality initiatives, it is believed, could maximize the effectiveness of investments aimed at improving the quality of care.

QRSs first emerged over a decade ago, in 1998, when the first such system was designed by the Child Care Division of the Oklahoma Department of Human Services. In response to concerns about the health and safety of children in child care and the preponderance of low-quality care, Oklahoma legislators called upon state leaders to develop Oklahoma's Reaching for the Stars program. This QRS defined four levels of quality with identified standards and indicators that licensed child care centers and family child care could voluntarily choose to address. Currently, 19 states (Colorado, Delaware, District of Columbia, Indiana, Iowa, Kentucky, Louisiana, Maine, Maryland, Mississippi, Montana, New Hampshire, New Mexico, North Carolina, Ohio, Oklahoma, Pennsylvania, Tennessee, and Vermont) have a statewide quality rating and improvement system (QRIS). In addition, at least 10 states either are implementing or are in the process of expanding pilot programs statewide. A number of localities including Los Angeles, California, and Miami-Dade and Palm Beach counties in Florida, are implementing QRISs within specific geographic areas or with certain types of programs (NCCIC, September 2009).

Common Elements of Quality Rating and Improvement Systems

QRSs generally address five elements of a systemic approach to quality improvement:

1. *Standards.* QRS standards are built on the foundation of child care licensing requirements and add multiple steps between licensing and higher quality standards, such as those associated with accreditation.

2. *Accountability measures.* Accountability and monitoring processes are used to determine how well programs meet system standards and to assign ratings.

3. *Program and practitioner outreach and support.* Support for providers, such as training, mentoring, and technical assistance, is included to promote participation and help programs achieve higher levels of quality.

4. *Financial incentives.* Financial incentives, such as tiered subsidy reimbursement [which pays a higher reimbursement rate to providers who care for children from families that receive subsidies from the Child Care and Development Fund (CCDF) of the U.S. Department of Health and Human Services and to providers who meet standards beyond minimum licensing], are awarded to programs when quality levels are achieved.

5. *Parent education efforts.* Most QRSs award easily recognizable symbols, such as stars, to programs to indicate the levels of quality and to inform and educate parents (Mitchell, 2005).

Challenges to Implementing Quality Rating Systems

The focus of early adopters of QRSs was on developing a system that would be quickly understood by parents and would result in increasing demand for, and consumer understanding of, the indicators of quality child care. The systems were established as mechanisms to ensure that public expenditures would support higher quality care. Subsequently, most early QRSs moved toward an increased focus on mechanisms and incentives for participation, retention, and improvement of practitioners and programs. Thus, "second-generation" (Satkowski, 2009) states and localities designing QRSs are building a significant focus on improvement into the governance and infrastructure of the system. The term *QRIS* is now more commonly used to describe this systemic approach to aligning quality initiatives.

It is no surprise that among the five "pioneer states" adopting a QRS (Oklahoma, Colorado, North Carolina, Pennsylvania, and Ohio) there was a common focus on staff training and education and on the classroom or learning environment. What states differed on was whether they included standards or indicators related to parent involvement, child–staff ratios, or national accreditation (Zellman & Perlman, 2008). Today, all 19 statewide QRSs include standards related to professional development, qualifications, and training—all of which represent a key touchstone for alignment with professional development systems. Many statewide QRSs also include standards related to learning and curriculum, parent and family involvement, administrative policies and procedures, and compliance with licensing (NCCIC, March 2009).

Considerable variation exists across QRSs in the specific standards or criteria used to assign ratings at each level within each of the core elements. Thus, although QRISs share common goals and purposes defined by the field, each state determines its own specific indicators and measures to track quality, methods to assign and monitor ratings, and provision of improvement supports. Variation among state QRSs is affected by a variety of factors, including costs and available resources, state goals and philosophies, licensing requirements, and the status of other quality improvement efforts.

QRSs were initially designed with a focus on child care programs, and today all 19 statewide systems also include Head Start programs and most also include family child care homes and prekindergarten programs. Although QRSs generally do not exclude infant–toddlers or school-age programs, few intentionally include criteria to address the specific needs of infant–toddler or school-age practitioners. For example, while most states include reference to the infant–toddler version of an environmental rating scale, just eight states define specific criteria for infant–toddler practitioners in standards (NITCCI, 2009), and 11 states embed or have stand-alone standards relevant to school-age practitioners (Afterschool Investments, January 2010).

The recent downturn in state economies has slowed the ability of state leaders to fund the start-up, scale-up, and sustainability of QRISs in order to reach significant numbers of practitioners and programs. The paucity of research on the validity and impact of QRSs, and the inadequacy of tools to measure and quantify important outcomes on programs or children have affected both costs and the resulting willingness and ability of state agencies to implement the more robust QRIS. States face a number of challenges in implementing QRSs, including whether to pilot the system, how to measure and monitor ratings, how to build public will and education, and how to ensure equitable access and persistence in improving quality over time.

States take different approaches to scaling up, from implementing the "full system" in one or more pilot communities, to implementing select components of the system. For example, Virginia developed standards for center-based programs to participate in the QRS and is currently piloting the system in select communities while the state has not yet had the funds to implement newly developed standards for family child care participation in the system; Kentucky piloted its QRS for child care centers and family child care homes in 17 counties before allowing the system to go statewide in 2001; and Rhode Island, currently piloting a QRS with early childhood centers and homes, will expand the pilot to include school-age providers in coming years (given the availability of funds).

Funding is a significant factor in the implementation of QRSs and often drives the approach taken to piloting, scale-up, and sustainability. Sufficient funding, especially in the "second-generation" QRISs, requires significant resources for incentives for participation and training and for strategies to support improvement and upward movement in the ratings. The costs of QRSs vary widely with the scope and scale of the programs they include, the measures and methods of rating and monitoring, and the types of program and practitioner supports that are utilized to support improvement (Stoney, 2004). Despite a short-term boost in resources available to administrators of CCDF due to American Recovery and Reinvestment Act funds, states that began to pilot or implement QRSs in the last few years are facing funding cutbacks, given the declines in state economies nationwide. As a result, the governance and operational structures of QRSs are expanding to include cross-agency partnerships, most commonly between the child care lead agency and the Department of Education, as in New Mexico, or between public agencies and private organizations or philanthropies, as in Virginia and Delaware.

Measuring and rating the quality of programs constitute the bedrock upon which the QRS rests. Without a set of indicators of quality that are understandable and meaningful to parents, the goal of QRSs to fuel consumer demand for quality care is thwarted. Well-defined and well-calibrated tiers, or levels, of quality, with reachable, but predictive, indicators of quality, are fundamental to an equitable and valid rating for practitioners and programs. These factors place significant demands on the measures used to assess program or provider quality and to measure its impact on children and youth. Unfortunately, the field of quality measurement in early childhood and school-age care is struggling to meet these demands. The most common tool used in statewide QRSs, is the Early Childhood Environment Rating Scale (ECERS) (Harms, Clifford, & Cryer, 1998) (including versions adapted for infant–toddler care, school-age care, and family child care). However, in recent years, policy makers, researchers, and others have raised a host of issues related to the method and frequency of use of environmental rating scales and to the reliability and validity of the ratings and results of the ECERS for the purposes and goals of QRSs (Tout et al., 2009).

To address these issues, new measures—notably, the Classroom Assessment Scoring System (CLASS), developed by Robert Pianta and colleagues (2008), and the Program Quality Assessment, developed by the High/Scope Educational Research Foundation (1998)—are being tested in some state QRSs. In addition, as states expand QRISs to address the needs of programs and practitioners serving a broad age range of children, indicators of staff quality and measures used to rate quality, for example, call for additional indicators within system elements. State leaders are increasingly becoming concerned with adequately addressing the quality of programs and practitioners serving diverse children, including children with special needs and children learning English.

Further, state legislators and other policy makers are not all convinced that a QRS is either a necessary or the right investment of public funds to improve quality. Three states—Oregon, Texas, and Utah—neither have nor are exploring the design of a QRS, in part due to resistance from state policy makers. Thus, parents, practitioners, and advocates need to be part of the design and implementation of QRSs to ensure that the system elements, standards, and criteria are relevant and aligned with the needs and resources of the state. These same players need to build public will and understanding of the goals of the QRS. It may take many years to gain political support and funding from legislators. For example, state policy makers and advocates in California have recently passed the Early

Learning Quality Improvement Act (Steinberg, 2009), and Los Angeles County has piloted a QRS since 2006. The bill establishes an advisory committee to recommend an early learning quality improvement system, including a quality rating scale; however, no funding is provided to support the mandate.

CURRENT NATIONAL LANDSCAPE OF PROFESSIONAL DEVELOPMENT SYSTEMS

Over the last 20 years, U.S. states and territories have funded multiple professional development activities offered by 4-year colleges and community colleges, extension services, Head Start, local school districts, and community-based child care agencies. Responding to participant demand and state and federal mandates, nearly all states have begun to develop a systems approach to planning and implementing professional development activities for their early care, early education, and school-age workforce. Although much of the research on the early care and education workforce applies to the school-age workforce as well, recent research has identified unique characteristics and a more refined understanding of the impact of professional development on those who work with school-age children. Research indicates that professional development improves quality and outcomes in school-age programs. Research has found positive associations between staff training and the academic motivation of youth and on-site coaching improved both staff skills and youth learning (Burkhauser & Metz, 2009).

Nearly all states fund one initiative that supports professional development at the systems level. All U.S. states and territories use CCDF quality and targeted funds to provide professional development activities. Fully 37 states use quality and targeted funds to build or support professional development systems, 24 are engaged in cross-system planning, and 21 are planning or implementing QRSs or tiered reimbursement systems. At least 30 states have credentials for individuals (not including teacher certification or licensure), and most of those have multiple credentials (NCCIC, July 2009, January 2010).

Common Elements of Professional Development Systems

Most systems of professional development have several interconnected components (Afterschool Investments, 2008; Lemoine, 2008):

Funding. Investment is needed to plan and implement professional development systems and to make training financially feasible for participants. Financial support for the system can include scholarships for professional development, courses, and degrees; compensation and retention initiatives; and tiered reimbursements or quality rewards as part of a quality rating improvement system.

Core knowledge and core competencies. These serve as the basis for professional development and include a career ladder to recognize and track progress.

Qualifications and credentials. These include degrees, preservice requirements, and continuing education requirements, among others.

Quality assurance. Training and trainers are monitored and evaluated to make sure that the training offered meets quality standards in both content and delivery. Activities in this domain include trainer and training approval systems.

Access and outreach. This component encompasses how providers and staff learn about and access training. Efforts in this area include the establishment of online databases of training and education opportunities, career development advisement, and the provision of multiple delivery methods of training (e.g., distance learning, workshops, mentoring programs).

Infrastructure to support the system. This includes a stable governance structure, effective leadership, adequate planning, and technical assistance expertise. State activity in this area has increased recently, with the help of funding from State Early Childhood Comprehensive Systems grants and Head Start–mandated State Advisory Councils on Early Childhood Education and Care.

As professional development systems evolve, states are adding components, expanding participation, and including more sectors. They are addressing governance, infrastructure, automation, and data maintenance needs. They are beginning to evaluate components and targeted initiatives. Further, they are attempting to link and align their professional development activities with early learning guidelines, core knowledge and competencies, and trainer–training approval systems. States with existing professional development and QRSs are seeking ways to align those systems.

Challenges to Implementing Professional Development Systems

States face significant challenges when they attempt to align the elements, standards, and quality assurance mechanisms of professional development systems with those in quality rating improvement systems and licensing systems. In attempting to meet these challenges, states are seeking to make investments that lead to a more skilled and stable workforce, improved programs, increased parental access to high-quality programs, and positive child outcomes. States also are looking for consistent methods to integrate coaching and mentoring activities as recognized components of professional development systems. For example, *relationship-based professional development*, a component of the access and outreach element of a professional development system, refers to the various professional development approaches that use relationships to foster change and facilitate quality improvement. States use a variety of titles and descriptions for relationship-based professional development, including *coaching, mentoring, consultation*, and *technical assistance*. Recent research supports the notion that intensity, continuity, and individualization affect the efficacy of a professional development program. Central to all types and definitions of relationship-based professional development is the relationship between the highly skilled professional and the less experienced or skilled professional. Differences among the various approaches are based on the type of relationship, the purpose of the activity, and how information is shared between the expert and client (NCCIC, May 2009b; Weber & Trauten, 2008).

Policy makers designing professional development systems must pay particular attention to developing the skills of family friends and neighbors, or "informal" providers, as they are the ones who care for a large percentage of children in subsidized child care settings in many states. Creating universal access to professional development activities and movement along a career pathway through the articulation of training, courses, or degrees is an important component of ongoing professional development systems work in the majority of states. In addition, states are struggling to ensure the availability of content-specific training for infant–toddler, school-age, and special-needs training; training in administration; and training of English-language learners and distance-learning opportunities for providers across the early childhood education spectrum. Providing a continuum of professional development opportunities for all roles, in all settings, and across sectors avoids duplication of effort, and developing governance and infrastructure policies that support the delivery of services across sectors is increasingly at the forefront of professional development systems planning efforts (NCCIC, 2008). States are beginning to conduct evaluations of these systems and their components to determine their effectiveness, outcomes, and efficiencies (Weber & Trauten, 2008).

Touchpoints Between Quality Rating Systems and Professional Development Systems: Opportunities to Strengthen System Integration

System building entails the connecting of related initiatives, policies, and practices into a coherent whole that allows greater access, efficiency, and effectiveness. The degree of integration (and thus the connection among elements) and the strength of the overall system relies on the "health" of each of the subsystems that make up the whole. So, for example, a QRS takes the licensing system and the professional development system and marries them to a rating or accountability system to bring all four systems' subsystems together with the aim of achieving a common goal: improved quality of care and better outcomes for children. Therefore, the intersection or integration, or absence thereof, of QRSs and professional development systems rests upon the robustness of a myriad of different subsystems, including licensing, accreditation, funding, and more. Consequently, opportunities to strengthen system integration lie in these subsystems, some of which are discussed next.

Licensing   What is the current role of licensing in early care and education? Traditionally, licensing's goal has been health and safety. After the enactment of the Child Care and Development Block Grant in 1990, some states beefed up their regulatory system to begin to address quality, paying particular attention to adult–child ratios, preservice and continuing training, and professional development. As more states move to implement quality rating improvement systems, they start at very different places vis-à-vis licensing. States whose licensing law is considered minimal often choose to use a licensed status as the "floor" of their system. In some cases, simply having a legal licensed status does not even get a provider to the first level—licensing "plus"—of a quality rating improvement system.

Over the past 20 years, a number of states have changed their licensing law to require that significant standards be met which support quality—for example, increased adult–child ratios, increased preservice staff training and education, and significant continuing professional development. In these cases, planning and implementing a quality rating improvement system requires a revamping of licensing requirements and, often, a redistribution of licensing resources and personnel to support both the emerging system and existing professional development resources (e.g., child care resource and referral centers, training subsidies).

Certification and Accreditation   It is likely that states which have instituted accreditation of some kind use that accreditation to meet a high-level standard in their quality rating improvement system (assigning a 4 or 5 in a five-star system). State systems differ on whether they will accept accreditation from either the National Association for the Education of Young Children or the National Association for Family Child Care as meeting their highest level within a quality rating improvement system. Teacher certification is an essential element in any early childhood education professional development or quality rating improvement system. When states have attempted to develop a cross-sector system of either kind, a particular challenge they have faced is aligning the usually higher standards for teachers in prekindergarten, Head Start, and early intervention programs with a system of professional development support that also includes child care providers.

Higher Education   Higher education plays the central role in early childhood and school-age teacher certification. Two- and four-year institutions have been involved to different degrees in the preservice and ongoing professional development of classroom teaching assistants, family child care and after-school providers, and providers who are family friends or neighbors. Often, higher education plays a key role in the assessment element of state quality rating improvement systems (e.g., conducting Early Childhood Environmental Rating Scales) (Harms, Clifford, & Cryer, 1998). Some states contract with colleges and universities to perform this task.

Training and Trainers   Training of child care providers who are not certified teachers takes place in a variety of settings: higher education (usually community colleges), child care resource and referral centers, and existing community-based agencies such as the Red Cross, youth development agencies, school districts, and Head Start programs. The individuals who train these providers also vary widely and come to the task with different degrees of preparation themselves, usually because state requirements for such trainers vary widely with licensing law, teacher certification systems, and existing program accountability measures. Some states have worked on establishing a professional development system that includes standards for such trainers, usually through a training registry and sometimes through trainer credentials (NCCIC, May 2009a).

   In implementing a quality rating improvement system, it is helpful if an existing training–trainer registry exists and can interface with the system, making it easy to assess a provider's or program's training history. A trainer registry or certification can play an important role in a quality rating improvement system when the system's standards are aligned with the registry or certification.

THE STATUS OF THE INTERSECTION AND INTEGRATION OF SYSTEMIC QUALITY IMPROVEMENTS

As states and localities have designed, implemented, and scaled up QRSs and professional development systems, a new understanding of the key factors that affect program quality and teacher effectiveness is emerging. These factors fall primarily along two dimensions of relevance to the intersection of all the systemic quality improvement efforts:

- *Access* to relevant education, training, and support necessary to meet the needs of a diverse workforce, to ensure that all individuals have equitable opportunities to access appropriate training, education, and support and are afforded incentives to complete needed training to improve their skills and knowledge.

- *Application* of the key elements of QRSs and professional development systems to specific program settings. Among these key elements are adaptations to ensure that programs and practitioners serving increasingly diverse groups of children are relevant and effective.

As research has become more robust on both the short- and long-term impacts of quality early care and school-age settings on outcomes for children and youth, the urgency of demands facing state leaders has increased. There is a pressing need for quality improvement systems, such as professional development systems and QRSs, to be aligned and integrated with one another, with key intersection points strongly coupled to ensure that all children realize expected outcomes. As a result, QRSs and professional development systems are pushing their current boundaries to address

- *Broader age ranges.* Whereas such systems used to focus primarily on children ages 3–5, they are now increasingly focusing on a broader development age range, including paying attention to the specific needs of infants, toddlers, and school-age children.

- *Broader types of settings.* Whereas such systems used to focus primarily on child care settings, they are now increasingly focusing on programs and practitioners in a wider range of settings, including Head

Start, school-based prekindergarten, and school-based and community-based school-age programs.

- *Broader characteristics of practitioners.* Whereas such systems used to focus primarily on child care providers with high school degrees but little further higher education, they are now increasingly focusing on providers with degrees or with some community college experience and are expanding their focus to include fields other than early childhood, including youth and recreation backgrounds.

The unfolding of professional development systems and QRSs has occurred primarily on parallel trajectories, with much variation in states along a number of factors: which system (i.e., professional development or QRS) is started first, the purpose and focus of each of the systems, the strength of the infrastructure of each system, and the degree of "coupling" among the elements of each system. As states and localities design and implement QRSs and professional development systems as subsystems within the infrastructure of the early care and education system, natural intersections become evident, though not always explicit.

As defined earlier, the core elements of a QRS and a professional development system generally address similar functions, albeit from slightly different perspectives. Although the language used to describe each element may be different for each system, the definitions and implications for programs, practitioners, and policy makers represent both common understandings and cross-cutting issues that affect the integration and intersection of the systems. In order to have an impact on teacher effectiveness, program quality, and outcomes for children and youth, system infrastructures must be designed so as to answer the following questions:

- *What are practitioners and programs expected to know and do?* Standards in a QRS and core knowledge and competencies in a professional development system enable all practitioners to have the necessary and sufficient skills to ensure the safety of the children in their care and the quality of the learning environment. Fundamentally, standards define the set of skills and requirements necessary to *enter* the system and the *pathway* needed to improve and to move up in the system.

- *How is the system accountable to the public?* Reliable and valid measures and benchmarks ensure that the system is implemented consistently: that participants are treated fairly and equitably, that expected outcomes are achieved, and that public funds are used efficiently and effectively. Accountability and quality assurance mechanisms define how standards are monitored and identify and track results.

- *What strategies allow providers to enter the system, progress through it, and be successful?* Program and practitioner outreach and support address the strategies (e.g., *training, mentoring*) to support practitioners who are entering and moving up the QRS. Access and outreach include strategies to help practitioners learn what kinds of training are available to them and to help them keep track of the training they have completed in the professional development system. This element most directly addresses the link between QRSs and professional development systems and could be considered the focal point, or at least starting point, for integration of the systems.

- *What is being financed? How much does it cost? What resources are available? What gaps exist? What sources of funding could be used?* In these difficult economic times, policy makers must develop a clear idea of what needs to be funded, including answering questions such as "For how many?" and "Over what time frame?" Increasingly, policy makers are examining all the resources available to improve quality, including existing state initiatives such as child care resource and referral centers, program improvement grants, accreditation facilitation projects, and tiered reimbursement to develop strategic financing plans that support integrated quality rating improvement systems and professional development systems.

A Framework for a Common Language for Building Systems of Quality Improvement

One way to encourage greater alignment and move the field toward a more tightly integrated system of quality improvement would be to share a common language and understanding of the elements that make up the system, In this regard, clear definitions must apply to each system and intersections between system elements must be identified. We offer the framework shown in Figure 1 to guide states and territories as they attempt to build and refine more integrated quality rating and improvement systems and professional development systems within the early care and education system. The framework identifies the core elements of a quality improvement system, and proposes definitions that help to align similar elements within quality rating and improvement systems and professional development systems. The framework could help states examine the degree of integration and intersection across system elements, with the goal of identifying gaps and opportunities to strengthen the touchpoints across subsystems.

Cross-cutting elements
Core elements, Quality Rating and Improvement System (QRIS)
Core elements, Professional development (PD)

GOVERNANCE

- Is a coordinating body that is broadly representative of key stakeholders
- Serves to establish a common vision and goals
- Functions as the nexus of partnerships and collaborative efforts to build a coordinated system
- Has authority to make policy and funding decisions

QRIS governance includes:
- Key leaders/partners designing and overseeing the system
- A process for oversight of ongoing operations, policy development, and long-term strategic planning.
- Broad stakeholder representation, including members of the PD system governance body

PD system governance includes:
- A stable governance structure
- Oversight of ongoing operations, policy development, and long-term strategic planning
- Broad stakeholder representation, including members of the QRIS governance body

STANDARDS

- Define what it takes to enter the system (i.e., licensing or other entry qualifications).
- Define what the expectations for practitioners and programs are at each level of the system.
- Identify staff qualifications and core competencies, appropriate curricula, outreach to parents, and other key topics.
- Align with identified outcomes for children/youth.

QRIS standards include:
- Licensing standards as the base of the system
- Two or more levels of standards beyond licensing, with incremental progressions to the highest level of quality as defined by the state
- Standards based on research about the characteristics of programs that produce positive child outcomes

PD system standards include:
- Core knowledge and core competencies, qualifications, and credentials
- Core content and a career ladder to recognize and track practitioner progress
- Credentials and degrees, preservice requirements, and continuing education requirements

SYSTEM FINANCING

- Supports the system, including the costs of standards, ongoing communication and collaboration, and costs associated with scaling up implementation
- Provides practitioner supports and incentives

QRIS funding includes:
- Incentives to improve learning environments, attain higher ratings, and sustain long-term quality. All statewide QRISs provide financial incentives of some kind.
- Higher reimbursement rates linked to the CCDF child care subsidy system, bonuses, quality grants, or merit awards
- Loans linked to quality ratings
- Priority given to applications for practitioner wage initiatives, scholarships

Figure 1.   Toward a common language for building systems of quality improvement.

PD systems funding includes:
- Scholarships for professional development, courses, and degrees
- Compensation and retention initiatives
- Tiered reimbursements or quality rewards in a QRIS

COMMUNICATIONS
- Online and print media, as well as conferences
- Coordination with key partners for the purpose of increasing access and building public support
- Supporting effective coordination with other elements of the system

QRIS parent education efforts include:
- A framework for educating parents about the importance of quality
- Easily recognizable symbols, such as stars, to programs to indicate the levels of quality and inform and educate parents
- Strategies to promote QRIS through media, posters, banners, certificates, decals, pins, and other items that are displayed by rated programs

PD access and outreach include:
- Methods that help providers and staff learn about and access trainings
- Online databases of training and education opportunities
- Distance-learning opportunities

ACCOUNTABILITY SYSTEMS
- Identify benchmarks and outcomes
- Have an integrated data system to track indicators for individuals, programs, and systems monitoring
- Are used to track both short- and longer term trends for ongoing system improvements

QRIS accountability and monitoring processes include:
- Indicators to determine how well programs meet QRIS standards
- Ratings, and approaches to verify ongoing compliance
- Benchmarks for measuring quality improvement to provide a basis of accountability for programs, parents, and funders by creating

PD quality assurance/trainer and training approval systems include:
- Registries or other systems to monitor and evaluate trainers and training to ensure that content and delivery meet quality standards.

PRACTITIONER SUPPORT, ACCESS, AND OUTREACH:
- Strategies to reach out to practitioners and programs to ensure equitable access
- A cohesive set of professional development and training opportunities

QRIS program/practitioner outreach and support includes:
- Assigning a mentor or coach to a program to facilitate the rating process
- Forming partnerships with existing providers of technical assistance in the State, such as child care resource and referral (CCR&R) agencies; programs participating in the QRIS may be given priority to receive this assistance
- Investing in specialized technical assistance, such as support regarding caring for infants and toddlers or integrating children with special needs

PD practitioner supports include:
- Career development advising
- Multiple delivery methods of training: distance learning, workshops, and coaching and mentoring programs
- A comprehensive range of supports from access, to persistence, to mastery
- Articulation across settings and sectors

CONCLUSION

Quality rating and professional development systems are living systems and, as such, evolve over time, growing and changing as new policies, practices, and economic issues emerge in the states and communities within which those systems function. As we have detailed in this chapter, early developers of both systems are making adjustments to accommodate increased expectations from parents and policy makers. Certainly, much has been learned in the last decade, but currently there are more questions than answers that policy makers, researchers, and other stakeholders must address in order to truly realize the opportunity that QRSs and professional development systems offer to significantly enhance the effectiveness of teachers and to achieve hoped-for outcomes for children.

STUDY QUESTIONS

1. What are the five common elements of QRISs?

2. What is the main difference in focus between the QRSs of the states that were early adopters of such systems and those of the "second-generation" states and localities?

3. What are the six common elements of professional development systems?

4. What is the difference between licensing, on the one hand, and certification or accreditation, on the other, in early care and education?

REFERENCES

Afterschool Investments. (2008, September). *Building professional development systems for the afterschool field*. Retrieved May 18, 2009, from http://www.nccic.org/afterschool/pd_systems.pdf

Afterschool Investments. (2010, January). *Quick facts on school-age care: trends in quality rating and improvement systems*. Retrieved March 27, 2010, from http://nccic.acf.hhs.gov/afterschool/qris_trends.html

Burkhauser, M. & Metz, A. (2009, February). *Using coaching to provide ongoing support and supervision to out-of-school time staff: part 3 in a series on implementing evidence-based practices in out-of-school programs*. Washington, DC: Child Trends.

Child Trends. (2009, May). *What we know and don't know about measuring quality in early childhood and school-age settings care and education settings*. OPRE Issue Brief #1, Washington, DC: Office of Research, Planning and Evaluation, Administration for Children and Families.

Harms, T., Clifford, R.M., & Cryer, D. (1998). *Early Childhood Environment Rating Scale: Revised Edition.* New York: Teachers College Press.

High/Scope Educational Research Foundation (1998). *Program Quality Assessment Tool.* Retrieved June 29, 2009, from http://www.highscope.org/Content.asp?ContentId=116

LeMoine, S. (2008). *Workforce designs: A policy blueprint for state early childhood professional development systems.* Washington, DC: National Association for the Education of Young Children. Retrieved May 18, 2009, from http://www.naeyc.org/files/naeyc/file/policy/ecwsi/Workforce_Designs.pdf

Mitchell, A.W. (2005, July). *Stair steps to quality: A guide for states and communities developing quality rating systems for early care and education.* Alliance for Early Childhood Finance for the United Way of America, Success By 6, and Collins Management Consulting, Inc.

National Child Care Information and Technical Assistance Center (NCCIC). (2008, December). *Professional development, staff qualifications, and/or training quality STANDARDS in QRS.* Retrieved May 18, 2009, from http://nccic.acf.hhs.gov

National Child Care Information and Technical Assistance Center (NCCIC). (2009). *Early childhood professional development toolkit.* Retrieved May 18, 2009, from http://nccic.acf.hhs.gov

National Child Care Information and Technical Assistance Center (NCCIC). (2009, March). *QRS quality standards.* Retrieved May 18, 2009, from http://nccic.acf.hhs.gov

National Child Care Information and Technical Assistance Center (NCCIC). (2009a, May). *Professional development system trainer and/or training approval systems.* Retrieved May 18, 2009, from http://nccic.acf.hhs.gov

National Child Care Information and Technical Assistance Center (NCCIC). (2009b, May). *Relationship based professional development: models, qualifications, training, and supports.* Retrieved May 18, 2009, from http://nccic.acf.hhs.gov

National Child Care Information and Technical Assistance Center (NCCIC). (2009, July). *State professional development activities quick facts.* Retrieved March 30, 2010, from http://nccic.acf.hhs.gov

National Child Care Information and Technical Assistance Center (NCCIC). (2009, September). *QRIS definitions and statewide systems.* Retrieved March 27, 2010, from http://nccic.acf.hhs.gov/pubs/qrs-defsystems.html

National Child Care Information and Technical Assistance Center (NCCIC). (2010, January). *State professional development system credentials for individuals.* Retrieved March 30, 2010, from http://nccic.acf.hhs.gov

National Child Care Information and Technical Assistance Center (NCCIC). (2010, March). *Use of environmental rating scales in quality rating systems.* Retrieved March 29. 2010, from http://nccic.acf.hhs.gov

National Infant-Toddler Child Care Initiative (NITCCI) (2009, March). *State quality rating and improvement systems (QRIS): Inclusion of infant/toddler indicators.* Washington, DC: author.

Pianta, R., Paro, K., & Hamre, B. (2008). *Classroom assessment scoring system.* Retrieved June 29, 2009 from http://www.classobservation.com/index.php

Satkowski, C. (2009, April). *A stimulus for seccond-generation QRIS.* New America Foundation, Washington, DC.

Steinberg, D. (2009). *Early Learning Quality Improvement Act SB 1629.* Retrieved March 27, 2010, from http://www.preschoolcalifornia.org/assets/pc-documents/sb-1629-steinberg-fact-sheet.pdf

Stoney, L. (2004, September). *Financing quality rating systems: Lessons learned*. Alliance for Early Childhood Finance for the United Way of America, Success By 6.

Tout, K., Zaslow, M., Halle, T., & Forry, N. (2009, May). *Issues for the next decade of Quality Rating and Improvement Systems*. OPRE Issue Brief #3, Washington, DC: Office of Research, Planning and Evaluation, Administration for Children and Families.

Weber, R.B., & Trauten, M. (2008, October). *Effective investments in the child care and early education profession: A review of the research literature*. Oregon Partnership Research Project, Oregon State University, Family Policy Program. Retrieved May 18, 2009, from http://www.hhs.oregonstate.edu/hdfs/sites/default/files/Lit_Review.pdf

Zaslow, M., Tout, K., Halle, T., & Forry, N. (2009, May). *Multiple purposes for measuring quality in early childhood settings: Implications for collecting and communicating information on quality*. (OPRE Issue Brief No. 2, Publication No. 2, 2009-13) Washington, DC: Child Trends. Retrieved June 6, 2009, from http://www.childtrends.org/Files//Child_Trends-2009_5_20_RB_MultPurposes.pdf

Zellman, G.L. & Perlman, M. (2008). *Child care Quality Rating and Improvement Systems in five pioneer states: Implementation issues and lessons learned*. Santa Monica, CA: RAND Corporation.

3

Integrating Professional Standards for the Early Childhood Workforce: Putting the Pieces Together

Sarah LeMoine, Alison Lutton,
Davida McDonald, and Jerlean Daniel

Children and families are at the center of early childhood education. The early childhood perspective on education emphasizes the positive growth and development of all children from birth to age 8 across all of the developmental domains—the whole child. For young children, learning starts with warm, responsive relationships that anchor their facilitated explorations of the world around them.

Realizing our collective hopes and dreams for all of our children from birth to age 8 requires supporting their development in all of its aspects—from social and emotional, to physical, to early literacy, to approaches to learning, and more. Early childhood teachers strive to maximize this development and learning, in partnership with parents and communities that represent considerable diversity in culture, race, ethnicity, socioeconomic class, family composition, first language, and abilities. Partnerships between homes and early childhood settings, as well as among the multiple early childhood settings a child may attend, also are essential.

EFFECTIVE TEACHERS

Fulfilling the promise and joy of learning requires a thoughtful, intentional teacher who scaffolds what young children know and are able to do and openly embraces their curiosity. Early childhood teachers are critical decision makers. What they do throughout the day matters. Excellent teachers know the science of learning and have a range of teaching strategies at their disposal. They know what they are doing, why they select a particular action at a particular time for these specific children, and how to mediate their practice to serve the individual needs of each child—including ongoing assessment to enhance teaching and learning.

The core knowledge of effective teachers includes knowledge about child development; an understanding of how to build and nurture family and community relationships; child observation, documentation, and assessment; teaching strategies; and professional standards, guidelines, and ethics (Hyson, 2003). It also includes an understanding of the developmental progression of content areas such as math, science, and language acquisition and literacy, as well as a grounding in these content areas themselves. An effective teacher understands that the sociocultural context of each child's life affects the child's receptivity to, and use of, educational experiences.

Excellent teachers who have a firm grasp of the core knowledge base of early childhood education are, first and foremost, governed by a high level of intentionality. In short, to be an excellent teacher means being intentional. Excellent teachers *intentionally* create a caring community of learners; *intentionally* teach to enhance development and learning; *intentionally* plan curriculum to achieve important goals; *intentionally* respond to children with observations of what the children know, can do, and care about; *intentionally* assess children's development and learning; and *intentionally* establish reciprocal relationships with families (Copple & Bredekamp, 2009).

There are standards that embrace these principles of what it means to be an effective teacher, to teach effectively, and more. These standards delineate competencies that are designed and administered at the national, state, and local levels.

MULTIPLE SETS OF CORE COMPETENCIES

Professional development offerings and systems are built on the foundation of standards that delineate core knowledge and competencies for early childhood teachers. Based on these desired skills and knowledge areas, state professional development activities are aimed at providing effective preparation, development, and support. But this effort is complicated by disparate early childhood sectors (e.g., Head Start and Early Head Start, child care, prekindergarten, kindergarten through third grade, early intervention, and special education). Historically, the various sectors have had different expectations for educator knowledge and competencies, rather than a single set of professional standards delineated by role; thus, professional standards and requirements vary according to funding streams and type of program (LeMoine, 2008). The variety of settings and needs in the early education field have sometimes been described as a rich tapestry. Yet, for early childhood professionals, understanding professional requirements and supports, particularly across sectors, can be an overwhelming task that requires them to navigate a maze of options rather than a comprehensible career pathway.

HISTORICAL CONTEXT

A long history of national and state efforts contributed to how and why the sectors developed and delineated their own sets of standards and expectations. Particularly from the early 1900s on, events resulted in the mostly siloed establishment of teacher preparation and ongoing development in public schools, child care, Head Start, early intervention, and special education.

Early 1900s

By the 1920s, both researchers and educators began organizing nursery schools for young children, and by the end of that decade the National Association for Nursery Education (NANE) was established and had published *Minimum Essentials for Nursery Education*, which specified standards, including teacher expectations, for nursery schools (National Association for the Education of Young Children, 2001). In the 1920s and early 1930s, social scientists brought interdisciplinary concepts related to human development to national discussions and had a significant influence on the understanding of the fundamental needs related to child development. A new lexicon triggered a deeper understanding of the emotional needs of children, helping to establish an integrated emphasis on social and emotional development, in addition to numeracy and literacy. The first nursery school teacher training institutions included this emphasis in their training and textbooks (Lascarides & Hinitz, 2000). The 1930s and 1940s heralded the development and implementation of the Works Progress Administration (WPA), a key New Deal agency. During World War II, the WPA developed nursery schools and child care programs with a heavy focus on supporting working parents. During this time, the U.S. Office of Education (1943) publicized the importance of teachers with specialized training in child development and nursery school or kindergarten education.

Although many state teacher certification systems are more than a century old, early childhood became established as a distinct teacher certification area with its own specialized core knowledge and competencies during more recent decades (Angus, 2001). In 1937, only five states required schoolteachers to have any professional training beyond high school. Around the same time, researchers began to call for at least 2 years of teacher training beyond high school, the first university departments of education were founded, high school enrollments grew, and teacher training gradually moved from normal schools to colleges. The leaders of the kindergarten and nursery school movements were among the first to establish full college degree programs for teachers and became founders of Wheelock College, Lesley University, Bank Street College, and National-Louis University (Fraser, 2007).

Mid-1900s

Professional preparation programs for teachers in early intervention and special education developed along with efforts to establish the right for children with disabilities to be educated. The Training of Professional Personnel Act of 1959 (PL 86-158), as well as other significant pieces of federal legislation passed during the late 1950s through the 1960s, established training programs and support for professionals working with children with disabilities (U.S. Office of Special Education Programs, 2002).

By the 1960s, the majority of public school teachers held at least a bachelor's degree and normal schools became state teachers colleges and then were integrated into general state systems of higher education. The research and policy discussion shifted to a focus on the quality of teacher education programs, and on connections between education, diversity, and civil rights (Fraser, 2007).

At the same time, Congress established multiple programs related to reducing poverty and creating economic opportunity for all, including the pilot program of Head Start in 1964. There was a heavy emphasis on states' rights related to education, so the federal government trod lightly on its issuance of standards, especially in regard to the competency of teachers. In 1964, NANE reorganized as the National Association for the Education of Young Children (NAEYC). NAEYC continued NANE's focus on and support for early childhood educators and increased its efforts to influence and develop a national set of standards for early childhood professionals.

The Federal Interagency Day Care Requirements (FIDCR) also were established in the 1960s. An attempt to coordinate requirements across federal programs, FIDCR was enacted into law via the Economic Opportunity Act in 1968, and was a set of national standards that applied to any child care program receiving federal funds (Gold, 1980). FIDCR included very minimal standards for staff qualifications. The standards were created by the Congress and had the support of the federal administration until disagreements arose regarding the differing levels of quality in the states. FIDCR was rewritten a number of times in rapid succession, yet only a slightly modified version was included in Title XX of the Social Services Amendments of 1974. In 1981, after continued controversy, Congress finally voted to abolish the FIDCR standards (Morgan, 1982).

Late 1900s and On

In the early 1970s, some landmark court cases set the groundwork for what would become inclusive practices in least restrictive environments. In 1975, Congress passed Public Law 94-142, known today as the Individuals with Disabilities Education Act. This federal law guarantees a free, appropriate public education to each child with a disability. Increased attention to related teacher competencies then emerged, with the expectation that every state and locality would provide education for children with disabilities (OSEP, 2002).

The 1970s and 1980s saw a movement to establish guidelines for early childhood teachers that would eventually become commonly accepted, including the Child Development Associate (CDA) credential competencies and the NAEYC guidelines for the associate, initial licensure, and advanced degree programs. The CDA Consortium was created in the U.S. Department of Health, Education and Welfare in 1971 and was charged with developing the CDA credential. A decade later, the Head Start Act passed and specified guidelines for the training of Head Start teachers and aides. The guidelines included required progressions toward degrees. At the same time, NAEYC released *Early Childhood Teacher Education Guidelines for 4- and 5-Year Programs* (National Association for the Education of Young Children, 1982), which was followed in 1984 by position statements on nomenclature, salaries, benefits, and the status of the early childhood profession and *Guidelines for Early Childhood Education Programs in Associate Degree Granting Institutions* (National Association for the Education of Young Children, 1984).

In 1985, NAEYC established the Council for Professional Recognition, to administer the CDA credential. The Council became a freestanding organization in 1989. In the mid- to late 1980s, NAEYC also developed additional critical position statements that influenced expectations for early childhood educators, including developmentally appropriate practice; quality, compensation, and affordability; and a code of ethical conduct.

In 1990, Congress established the Child Care and Development Block Grant (CCDBG) Act, part of the Omnibus Budget Reconciliation Act of 1990 (PL 101-508). CCDBG was later amended by the Personal

Responsibility and Work Opportunity Reconciliation Act of 1996 (PL 104-193) and the Balanced Budget Act of 1997 (PL 105-33). Although CCDBG was passed by Congress with a focus on supporting low-income populations, it included required quality set asides that states used in part to fund professional development activities. This was the first major infusion of federal monies that states could use to support the preparation and development of the early childhood workforce. The funds supported the early building of professional development systems targeted at the child care workforce, but they also included supports for professionals in each early childhood sector.

In 1990, NAEYC joined with the National Association of Early Childhood Specialists in State Departments of Education to write expectations regarding assessments of young children. NAEYC also published guidelines regarding early childhood educator compensation, tied to competencies. The National Institute for Early Childhood Professional Development was created in 1991, and 2 years later NAEYC's "Conceptual Framework for Professional Development" included the importance of an early childhood common core and competencies as a central theme (NAEYC, 1994). Wheelock College's Center for Career Development also was created during this time and supported states' professional development efforts with technical assistance and a system framework that included a call for state competencies for early childhood professionals (Morgan et al., 1993).

The 1990s saw the emergence of state-funded preschool or prekindergarten programs as well, distinct from state-subsidized child care and early intervention for children with disabilities. Research made the case for positive long-term outcomes for children who had access to quality preschool programs. By the end of the decade, the New Jersey Supreme Court ruled, in *Abbott v. Burke*, that the state must fund preschool for disadvantaged children in the poorest school districts. Also by the end of the decade, 40 states had state-funded preschool programs. Although there was considerable variability in quality, some states extended early childhood teacher certification where it was already in place for kindergarten, while experimenting with ways to include community child care and Head Start programs in the prekindergarten mix (Barnett, Brown, & Shore, 2004; Barnett, Epstein, Friedman, Boyd, & Hustedt, 2008).

In 1998, Congress passed the Community, Opportunities, Accountability, and Training and Educational Services (COATES) Act, which reauthorized Head Start through 2003. COATES included the mandate that 50 percent of Head Start teachers earn at least an associate's degree in early childhood education or a related field by 2003. National figures showed that not only was this target achieved, but it was surpassed. Between 1999 and 2002, there was a 14 percent increase in the percentage of Head Start teachers with college degrees. Approximately 23% attained an associate's degree, 25% earned a bachelor's degree, and 4% completed graduate degrees. Nationally, the 50% goal was attained, but variability by state indicated that access to early childhood education degree programs was a challenge, especially in many rural areas (U.S. Government Accountability Office, 2003).

With the development of separate standards and infrastructures for the major early childhood sectors, states and teachers were, and in many cases still are, overwhelmed by the daunting task of navigating the related multiple processes for professional preparation and ongoing development (Marzano & Kendall, 1998). However, at the same time, all of this increased attention and activity was central to the building of some national consensus on the competencies and standards for early childhood professionals. Although the individuality of states made the requirement of national standards improbable, if not impossible, voluntary national guidelines both influenced and were influenced by the competency work of the states.

The past two decades have seen the continued development of state competencies and systems that deliver related training and education, again guided by national standards and emerging research. Despite cross-sector committees involved in the development of many state competencies, the delivery mechanisms, content, and associated roles on career lattices often continue to be segregated by program settings and funding streams. The three major early childhood sectors—child care, Head Start, and public schools—typically continue to set their own expectations and competencies for early childhood teachers working in their individual sectors.

Child Care Core Knowledge and Competencies   Unlike other early childhood education sectors (e.g., Head Start, public schools), the child care segment of the workforce has not had an institutionalized infrastructure for professional development. To satisfy this need, many states created systems of support targeted specifically at that sector. At least 50% of states have developed specific core knowledge and competencies, targeted predominantly at the child care sector workforce, with many using categories from either or both of the CDA credential competencies and the NAEYC professional preparation standards (LeMoine, 2009). State core knowledge and competencies often serve as a foundation for community-based training and methods to organize, publicize, and track these professional development offerings. Training in core knowledge areas is intended to provide both targeted development and incremental stepping-stones from minimum requirements in licensing regulations to higher education courses and degrees. In their child care licensing requirements, states typically include multiple qualification alternatives for child care staff. Within these alternatives, only 13 states require center-based teachers to have any early childhood education preservice qualifications, 9 require such qualifications of small family child care providers, and 15 require them of large family child care providers. However, 48, 38, and 37 states require center-based teachers, small family child care providers, and large family child care providers, respectively, to have ongoing training (National Child Care Information and Technical Assistance Center, 2007a, 2007b). Of the states that require ongoing training for center-based teachers, 75% also specify training content areas (National Child Care Information and Technical Assistance Center & National Association for Regulatory Administration, 2009). In these regulations, no state requires or encourages teachers to get college credit for their ongoing training, but many teachers do take college courses anyway, for a variety of reasons.

Many states worked to align or develop child-care–focused core knowledge and core competencies tied specifically to early learning guidelines. Since 2002, the Good Start, Grow Smart initiative (the early childhood companion to the No Child Left Behind Act of 2001, PL 107-110) has encouraged states to develop and implement early learning guidelines for young children, as well as provide related professional development and training. Although states' work to delineate early learning guidelines preceded this initiative, a renewed emphasis on the development of these standards resulted from it. Good Start, Grow Smart includes reporting requirements in states' biennial Child Care and Development Fund plans on progress in developing the guidelines and in state plans for professional development.

Head Start Core Knowledge and Competencies   Early childhood professionals in Head Start and Early Head Start programs work to meet requirements specified in the Head Start performance standards, which include staff qualifications. In addition to satisfying specific educational and experience requirements, these professionals must meet general requirements which specify that "Grantee and delegate agencies must ensure that staff and consultants have the knowledge, skills, and experience they need to perform their assigned functions responsibly" (Office of Head Start, 2008). The 2007 reauthorization of Head Start requires that by 2013 all Head Start teachers will have completed at least an associate's degree and that 50 percent of those teachers will have earned a bachelor's degree in early childhood education.

Public School Core Knowledge and Competencies   Competencies required for public school teachers are codified in state teacher certification or licensure requirements for individual teachers and in state systems that approve teacher education degree programs that lead to certification. Teacher education programs in public institutions of higher education are approved and funded to prepare graduates for certification in areas needed in the state in which they operate. State teacher certification requirements generally include the successful completion of a state-approved teacher education program at the baccalaureate level, a specific grade point average, and a minimum passing score on a state-selected standardized exam in the teacher's specialty. State certification typically begins at a provisional level and requires a number of years of successful teaching practice and continuing professional development in order to earn permanent or advanced certification.

States define early childhood and related certifications in a variety of ways: birth to 5 years old, prekindergarten to third grade, and nursery school to fourth grade. Although the great majority of states that recognize or require early childhood certification have aligned their early childhood teacher standards with NAEYC standards, the age range defined is likely to affect the core knowledge and competency areas that are emphasized in each state.

Intentionally or not, siloed sector requirements and professional development efforts have created institutionalized barriers which detrimentally affect the workforce that various systems are designed to support. At the heart of this problem is a lack of coordination across programmatic sectors, due in large part to varying funding streams and infrastructures. These barriers to career development have been troubling teachers, administrators, trainers, teacher educators, policy makers, and researchers in the early childhood field for decades. They grow only more pressing as we gain a clearer understanding of where the field is headed in the first decades of the 21st century.

APPROACHING INTEGRATION

The various sectors' collection of sponsoring and regulating agencies that create a mosaic of priorities, policies, and expectations regarding the training, education, and credentialing of early childhood professionals lead to a number of challenges. One great challenge currently and for the next decade and beyond is for states to work toward integration of the expectations, competencies, and requirements for early education professionals regardless of the setting or the states' funding stream. At the local, state, and national level, often the question is not "Should we work to align competencies?" but "Is it possible to align competencies across all of these sectors?"

Unified Standards

All of the early care and education programs and settings exist, at least in part, for the purpose of promoting the development and learning of young children from birth to age 8. The science of child development provides a base for defining what young children need, regardless of the setting in which they spend their days. This developmental perspective emerged in the early 1900s and continues to gain support today in the field of education, from NAEYC's newly revised *Developmentally Appropriate Practices on Early Childhood Programs Serving Children from Birth Through Age 8* (Copple & Bredekamp, 2009) to the National Council for Accreditation of Teacher Education's (NCATE) (n.d.) project to apply the science of child development to standards for all teacher education programs from prekindergarten to grade 12 and the Association for Supervision and Curriculum Development's (2007) Whole Child Initiative.

This effort to better integrate knowledge of child development into training and education for all teachers can provide common ground for defining an integrated set of professional standards that includes a cross-sector core of knowledge and competencies for early childhood professionals that might also be shared across states.

Early learning standards for young children can, and often do, inform what we want early childhood professionals to know, understand, and be able to do. If such standards are developed by putting children's needs first, they provide a common framework that integrates child care, Head Start, and prekindergarten through third grade.

The 2001 revisions to NAEYC's standards for early childhood professional preparation programs effected a conceptual shift toward standards that express a shared professional vision of what tomorrow's early childhood teachers should know and be able to do. Meeting these standards requires an examination of student performance on key assessments aligned with key elements—knowledge, understanding, and practice—for each standard.

Unified Standards as a Basis for Integrated Professional Development Systems

Integrated professional development systems are careful to include higher education programs as essential partners on the continuum of career development. Higher education can build early childhood degree programs to meet and integrate state certification requirements, state quality rating and improvement system (QRIS) criteria, Head Start national standards, and more. They can and should be an important part of state professional development systems. Those who have earned early childhood degrees should share a common foundation of professional knowledge and practice that can be applied to multiple settings, roles, and age groupings over the course of a career.

As states undertake system integration efforts, planners also must proactively address the complicating factor that segments of society may not have access or support to obtain professional development, particularly within higher education degree programs. Plans must help the early educa-tion field understand how a teacher can work with young children while pursuing a career progression leading to a degree. In order to build an early childhood workforce that is both diverse and well qualified, special atten-tion needs to be paid to the recruitment and retention of suitable individu-als and to their successful completion of degree programs. Among adults age 25 and older in the United States today, only 31% of Whites, 19% of Blacks, and 10% of Hispanics have obtained bachelor's degrees (U.S. Department of Commerce, 2005). This reality is reflected in the current demographics of the early childhood workforce. For example, the percent-age of White teachers in California rises as degree requirements and salaries rise, from 63% of child care workers to 78% of preschool teachers and 82% of elementary and secondary school teachers. The figures are most striking for Latino teachers: 16.5% of child care teachers, and just 6% of preschool and elementary and secondary school teachers are Latino (Chang, 2006). The strongest teacher education programs not only are aligned with professional standards, but also demonstrate responsiveness to the needs of their unique students and communities (Lutton, 2009).

Without deliberate collaboration and attention to unintended conse-quences, competency systems can create barriers to the full development of an individual teacher's professional career. If higher education degree programs are too narrow, the teacher may need to return to college in order to move to a new setting or age group within the early childhood field. If these programs do not include intentional, targeted access and support, they will not reflect the diversity of the field. If state agencies do not collaborate on early care and early education competencies and cre-dentials, training hours and credentials earned may not count if the teacher moves from a child care center to a school-based classroom. Unless states make efforts to align with national standards and develop reciprocity agreements, professional credentials may not be recognized when a teacher moves to a new state. Unless training and higher education standards are aligned, training hours are not likely to articulate into col-lege credits.

Intentional systems integration efforts not only benefit the workforce and, ultimately, the children and families they serve, but also can result in financial and other savings at individual, programmatic, and system levels. Integrated policies intentionally promote the building and support of an efficient cross-sector system that decreases duplication of efforts and increases sustainability.

State policies should establish an integrated system of professional development based on consistent professional standards across the early childhood sectors: child care, Head Start, prekindergarten, public schools, early intervention, and special education. Among the essential

policies that connect professional development elements and components and that support and make possible a state system of professional
development are policies on professional standards, career pathways,
articulation, an advisory structure, data, and financing. These policies
should be embedded into the early care and education system with
appropriate rules, regulations, and statutes in all the agencies that over-
see or administer each sector. Policies also should be embedded in other
cross-sector activities that touch the workforce, such as QRISs
(LeMoine, 2008).

Integrated Professional Development Systems Are Key to State Quality Rating and Improvement Systems

Integrated professional development systems are an integral piece of
states' overarching quality improvement efforts, especially QRISs.
QRISs offer a unique opportunity to link professional standards across
the various sectors of the field. However, the linkages are only as
strong as the standards and supports that underlie them—meaning that
early childhood core competencies and professional development systems must be as comprehensive and integrated as possible. States and
localities develop and implement QRISs with the primary goal of
increasing the overall quality of early childhood programs and with an
additional focus on recognizing and rewarding programs that meet
increasingly higher levels of quality. QRISs can and do include a broad
range of early care and education settings (e.g., center- based child
care, family child care, school-age, prekindergarten, Head Start programs) and funding streams. Thus, they have the potential to link
across sectors to bridge early childhood regulations and program and
professional standards. QRISs share a set of common components, one
of which is the standards and criteria that are embedded within them. It
is through these standards and criteria that the linkages to early childhood education competencies and program standards are strengthened
(McDonald, 2009).

Since the majority of QRISs are voluntary, the criteria that they
establish for what teachers should be taught, what teachers should know
and do, and which pieces of their knowledge base should be maintained
and expanded cannot be mandated through regulation. However, two
major opportunities arise for linking existing professional standards to a
QRIS, as well as to engage multiple stakeholders: the planning phase
and the implementation phase. Those who develop and administer quality rating and improvement systems should take full advantage of these
opportunities by including representatives from the various sectors of

the early childhood field throughout the planning and implementation phases.

One of the key tasks during the planning phase is determining which standards and criteria will be included in the QRIS. This task is typically undertaken by a planning group, which should include representatives from the various sectors of the early childhood field in order to ensure that standards and criteria truly link to existing program and professional standards. Planning groups also should engage representatives from the provider community, as well as end users—consumers—to ensure that the QRIS maintains a focus on provider and consumer education and outreach.

Through the opportunity afforded by the implementation phase, program evaluation data are collected and examined and those who administer the QRIS also review the standards and criteria—a type of continuous quality improvement for the system. As implementation proceeds, an advisory body can participate in the review of standards. That body can, and should be, as representative of the various sectors of the early childhood field as was the planning group. This intentional diversity can ensure strong linkages across the sectors and infrastructures the advisory body members represent—linking early learning standards, standards for all early childhood professionals, and the professional development system as well.

STATE EXAMPLES

More and more states are engaging in intentional system integration efforts. Increasingly, they are using the foundation of child standards as a basis for teacher competencies, teacher competencies as a basis for professional development systems, and integrated professional development systems as an integral part of QRISs and other quality improvement efforts. The discussion that follows highlights the intentional system building and integration work undertaken by two states: Connecticut and Pennsylvania. The authors are grateful to state representatives who informed these overviews.

Connecticut's Practitioner Pathways: A Fortuitous Collision

In Connecticut-Charts-A-Course, the state's early childhood professional development system, formed a work group to establish core competencies in the early 1990s. A concerted effort was made to align the competencies with the standards in the Child Development Associate (CDA) credential. The alignment was done in part to help the child care workforce meet state licensing requirements: Connecticut's state licensing agency had recently included a CDA credential or 12 credits in early childhood or child development, effective July 20, 1993, as a requirement for lead teachers in center-based programs (Regulations of Connecticut State Agencies, title19a).

Once the competencies and standards were aligned, the state still lacked a vehicle to deliver training based on the competencies. State prekindergarten had not yet been established, and professionals working in the system for kindergarten to third grade had to meet a different set of expectations required by state certification. This public school sector of the workforce was receiving education and development solely through higher education institutions.

In 1997, the year that Connecticut adopted its school readiness legislation (Connecticut General Statutes Annotated §10-16o), energies turned to developing a training program based on the competencies. The legislation that was adopted also resulted in an increased emphasis on aligning the previously developed competencies with the new NAEYC professional preparation standards. The publication of NAEYC's standards for associate's degree, initial licensure, and advanced degree programs in what became known as the "red book" encouraged the state to examine all of the existing standards. A work group examined the competencies and their relation to the CDA credential standards, the state's early childhood associate's and bachelor's degree standards, and teacher certification requirements. The examination, which was conducted to inform revisions to the competencies and the design of related training, included a focus on professionals' movement from one type of training to another, removing barriers to articulation.

Evaluations of the new competency-based training examined whether the programs were preparing professionals to obtain the CDA credential and to pass the state's Early Childhood Pathways exams. Through an agreement between Connecticut-Charts-A-Course and Charter Oak State College, credit for prior knowledge can be awarded to someone who passes these exams. Three exams can be taken for up to nine college credits, in Introduction to Early Childhood Education, Child Developmental Psychology, and Infant/Toddler Growth and Development. The exams, developed by faculty in the school's associate's and bachelor's degree programs, used content from the associate's degree level, under the assumption that that content was aligned with the NAEYC associate's degree standards as a measure of quality assurance. The initial tests were normed on students who had taken Introduction to Early Childhood Education and Child Developmental Psychology in an associate's degree program; faculty agreed to use the tests as their final exam in those two courses.

After norming, the exams were offered to all early childhood professionals. Data were gathered on whether the competency-based training was rigorous enough to help participants pass the exams. A majority—over 80 percent—of those who completed the 150-hour introductory training in early childhood education passed the related Pathways exam. However, less than half of the students who took the training in child development passed the exam.

With a national push for higher staff credentials, together with the opportunity for national accreditation of higher education institutions through NAEYC and the NCATE, Connecticut reexamined its overall professional development system. The state began to look across the systems and sectors, seeking opportunities for more uniformity and alignment, as well as ways to ensure articulation from one level of training and preparation to the next. Policy timing was ripe for this type of investigation and planning, as the state's early childhood cabinet also was pushing for scrutiny and alignment.

In 2005, with data gleaned from the Pathways exams and other research, as well as policy and national support, the system planners and the work group reexamined the core competencies. Rewriting them in their entirety, the two groups also standardized all of the accompanying training outlines, content, and trainer and delivery requirements. Recently, the Pathways exams were retooled; results are pending.

Connecticut describes its two systems—the competency system and the professional development system—as colliding. Pending legislation includes a requirement of a CDA credential *plus* 12 credits in early childhood education or child development for staff in any publicly funded program. The state Departments of Social Services and Education came to an agreement on this recommendation. Connecticut-Charts-A-Course's career ladder is now based on a 12-credit requirement, and any professional working in a program supported by public funds from the state Department of Social Services or the state Department of Education or from the federally funded Head Start must be in the state's professional development registry, which records professionals' qualifications and development according to the state competencies and related career lattice.

Linkages and alignment have made a significant difference for Connecticut's workforce, especially in terms of access to and successful completion of professional development that furthers an individual's credentials. New requirements for the state's early childhood teacher certification are being aligned with NAEYC professional preparation standards. All of the state's associate's degree programs are working toward accreditation. The state continues to look across all the different levels and standards for how it could align them, as it continues its efforts to support all of its early childhood professionals. (More information about

Connecticut's professional development system is available on the Internet at http://www.ctcharts-a-course.org.)

Pennsylvania's Cross-Sector Journey

Pennsylvania's early childhood professional development efforts for child care took root in the early 1990s, using a combination of federal funds from the Child Care and Development Fund and state general fund revenues. The work was organized through the Department of Public Welfare. Other early childhood state programs grounded in early intervention and public education had a stronger basis for the initial requirements for their sector's staff as well as for ongoing continuing education.

In 2000, the state developed a plan for a child care and early childhood training system. This plan included a call for several new professional development components and initiatives, including core knowledge areas. Again, like many other states, Pennsylvania developed its core body of knowledge by a cross-sector committee, which designed it exclusively for the child care workforce. A companion Professional Development Record also was developed to assist child care staff in planning and tracking their professional development in the areas covered in the core body of knowledge. A trainer quality assurance system and an online training calendar also were created, with the core body of knowledge used as a framework. All this work had many good elements, but it lacked both interconnections and requirements that would serve the entire early childhood education workforce, as well as essential connections to higher education, to public education, and to early intervention. In addition, it did not ensure, or even make it more likely, that more child care teachers and administrators would earn early childhood education degrees and credentials. Moreover, the plan was not organized to encourage or develop local and regional leadership and capacity.

Over the last few years, Pennsylvania has focused on revamping its early childhood programs and infrastructure, thanks to bold leadership and opportunities for policy changes. The Office of Child Development and Early Learning (OCDEL), a joint office of the Pennsylvania Departments of Public Welfare and Education, was established by Governor Ed Rendell to focus on early education and to develop a continuum of integrated early childhood services and a systematic approach to the provision of those services to Pennsylvania's children. OCDEL promotes opportunities for all Pennsylvania children and families by building systems and providing supports across all early learning sectors. To help implement this vision, the Pennsylvania Early Learning Keys to Quality initiative was created in 2005.

The goal of Early Learning Keys to Quality is to create a quality improvement system in which all early learning programs and practitioners are encouraged and supported to improve child outcomes. Improvements in programming are designed to increase the capacity to support children's learning and development, increase educational attainment among practitioners, and enhance professional skills and competencies in support of children's learning and development. The creation of the Early Learning Keys to Quality represented a major shift in organization and approach to supporting the early education workforce and the children and families the program serves. It has a cross-sector focus, with state, regional, and local governance structures.

The state's professional development elements from the 1990s have been updated, but in some instances are now being eliminated as the Commonwealth has continued to challenge the conventional thinking about the components of early education and how to best ensure integration and the creation of the necessary professional and service continuum. Among the new elements added to the state's professional development system was a cross-sector career lattice. Also advanced was an intentionally integrated approach to professional development and support within the core programs related to early education—specifically, Keystone STARS (the state's QRIS) and Pennsylvania Pre-K Counts.

Of the original professional development elements designed for child care, the core body of knowledge was revised in 2006 to use more inclusive, cross-sector language and to align with the early learning standards that recently had been created. For example, language was made more inclusive of public school staff when it was changed to say "directors/ administrators" rather than only "directors." References to the state's new early learning guidelines also were included, and core-body-of-knowledge requirements were incorporated into Keystone STARS. Even with these changes, the core body of knowledge continues to be used predominantly by child care staff; however, these initial steps laid important groundwork for the state's ongoing journey toward an integrated professional development system designed for all early childhood professionals.

In 2007, Pennsylvania revised its teacher certification requirements, known as Chapter 49-2, through its regulatory process. These significant revisions removed the state's omnibus K–6 teaching certificate, provided for either a prekindergarten–fourth-grade certificate or a fourth-to eighth-grade certificate, and changed the content of each certificate to include preparation for English-language learners, as well as children with special needs (Pennsylvania Administrative Code, Title 22). In addition, through its own internal administrative apparatus, the Department of Education improved the content approach for the certificates, thereby ensuring that they would meaningfully address child development, instructional content and practice, and assessment and accountability. These content guidelines were created by a cross-sector group that included significant leadership from OCDEL. The guidelines were distributed to institutions of higher learning in 2008, and institutions are currently submitting revised programs for approval by the Department.

With the passage of Section 49-2 of the Pennsylvania Administrative Code, the challenge became how the core body of knowledge could link with the new guidelines to create a more seamless system for practitioners' education and professional development. To address this challenge, OCDEL is planning to substitute the new content guidelines established throughout the teacher certification changes for the core body of knowledge. This substitution will provide integrated standards for all early childhood educators, ensuring the same content and approach through the early childhood professional development preparation and support processes.

Efforts are underway to revise the Professional Development Record to align it with the competencies incorporated into the new approach to teacher certification. With some additions and modifications, this body of work that is used to direct the efforts of higher education teacher preparation can then become the core body of knowledge for early childhood education practitioners. Because the work for teacher preparation in higher education is aligned with the NAEYC professional preparation standards, professional development for early childhood education practitioners would also be linked to those standards. Among the benefits of using the new content guidelines as the core body of knowledge are transparency for early childhood professionals, increased opportunities for professional development for college credit, and expanded opportunities for articulation. A single set of professional standards that includes levels and age-group specifications, as appropriate, can serve as a foundation for an integrated professional development system.

These focused and intentional integration efforts represent just one step of many that are left to take to provide for meaningful professional preparation and development and to make sure that any services provided are not siloed by the early childhood sectors. OCDEL also is finalizing its next 3-year professional development strategic plan, with a significant focus on true cross-sector supports that continue to improve the state's integrated approach for the teachers and administrators working in child care, prekindergarten, and early intervention. Through this planning process, Pennsylvania is examining new roles and requirements for supervisors, administrators, and other leaders and how these roles and requirements can be appropriately developed for the early learning system. (Additional information about Pennsylvania's system integration efforts is available on the Internet at http://www.pakeys.org. The guidelines contained in Section 49-2 of the Pennsylvania Administrative Code are available at http://www.pde.state.pa.us.)

PIECES OF THE PUZZLE

Integration is a challenging undertaking that is both a necessary and desirable goal for the early childhood field. When integration and alignment are lacking, there are policy discrepancies and dysfunctions. Since policy and systems change is often realized through incremental steps, intentional systems integration must be seen as a long-term goal that requires a broad vision, strong leadership, and a commitment to continuous improvement.

Early childhood educators play a pivotal role in the field, and the absence of unified standards and competencies for these teachers is a roadblock to truly integrated systems. Throughout the field's history, educators, researchers, advocates, and policy makers have worked in and across sectors at the local, state, and national levels to define the knowledge and skill base required of an effective teacher. The opportunity and the challenge early education faces in the next decade and beyond is to build more integrated state professional development systems that can offer stabilization for the field and support an individual's lifelong career in early childhood. Systems need to support integration while simultaneously advancing qualifications and encouraging standards that offer incentives for improvement. Aligned standards for licensing, funding, accreditation, and QRISs must be part of the mix. To be effective, state systems need to align with a framework of national standards, prepare professionals for the full early childhood age range, provide a foundation for work in a variety of settings, address specific state and community contexts, and be responsive to the needs of specific communities of adult learners. Integration efforts must continue, but in many states, most pieces of the puzzle are on the table.

STUDY QUESTIONS

1. What conceptual shift did the 2001 revisions to NAEYC's standards for early childhood professional preparation programs make?

2. What two phases of a QRIS offer major opportunities to link existing professional standards to the QRIS?

3. What steps did Connecticut take to ensure that its two systems—the competency system and the professional development system—would effectively "collide"?

4. How did Pennsylvania revise its core body of knowledge and teacher certification requirements to align better with early learning standards?

REFERENCES

Angus, D. (2001). *Professionalism and the public good: A brief history of teacher certification*. Washington, DC: Thomas B. Fordham Foundation.

Association for Supervision and Curriculum Development. (2007, March). ASCD calls for a "new compact" to educate the whole child. *Education Update, 49*(3).

Barnett, S., Brown, K., & Shore, R. (2004, April). The universal vs. targeted debate: Should the United States have preschool for all? *Preschool Policy Matters, 6*. New Brunswick, NJ: National Institute for Early Education Research.

Barnett, S., Epstein, D.J., Friedman, A.H., Boyd, J.S., and Hustedt, J.T. (2008). *The state of preschool 2008: State preschool yearbook*. New Brunswick, NJ: National Institute for Early Education Research.

Chang, H. (2006) *Getting ready for quality: The critical importance of developing and supporting a skilled, ethnically and linguistically diverse early childhood workforce*. Oakland, CA: California Tomorrow.

Connecticut General Statutes Annotated, Title 10, Education and Culture, Chapter 164, Educational Opportunities, Part I. General, §10-16o, Development of network of school readiness programs.

Copple, C., & Bredekamp, S. (Eds.). (2009). *Developmentally appropriate practice in early childhood programs serving children from birth through age 8* (3rd edition). Washington, DC: National Association for the Education of Young Children.

Fraser, J.W. (2007). *Preparing America's teachers: A history*. New York: Teachers College Press.

Gold, J. (1980). *Administration of the FIDCR: A description and analysis of the federal day care regulatory role* (Technical paper 2). Washington, DC: U.S. Department of Health, Education, and Welfare.

Hyson, M. (Ed.). (2003). *Preparing early childhood professionals: NAEYC's standards for programs*. Washington, DC: NAEYC.

Lascarides, V., & Hinitz, B. (2000). *History of early childhood education*. New York: Falmer Press.

LeMoine, S. (2009). [State child care professional development components]. Unpublished raw data.

LeMoine, S. (2008). *Workforce designs: A policy blueprint for state early childhood professional development systems*. Washington, DC: NAEYC.

Lutton, A. (2009). NAEYC early childhood professional preparation standards: A vision for tomorrow's early childhood teachers. In A. Gibbons & C. Gibbs (Eds.), *Conversations on early childhood teacher education: Voices from the working forum for teacher educators*. Redmond, WA: World Forum Foundation and New Zealand Tertiary College.

Marzano, R.J., & Kendall, J.S. (1998). *Awash in a sea of standards*. Aurora, CO: Mid-continent Research for Education and Learning.

McDonald, D. (2009). *Elevating the field: Using NAEYC early childhood program accreditation to support and reach higher quality in early childhood programs*. Washington, DC: NAEYC.

Morgan, G. (1982). *The FIDCR fiasco*. Unpublished teaching materials. Boston: Wheelock College.

Morgan, G., Azer, S., Costley, J., Genser, A., Goodman, I., Lombardi, J., et al. (1993). *Making a career of it: The state of the states report on career development in early care and education*. Boston: Wheelock College, Center for Career Development in Early Care and Education.

National Association for the Education of Young Children. (1982). *Early Childhood teacher education guidelines for 4- and 5-year programs* (position statement). Washington, DC: Author.

National Association for the Education of Young Children. (1984). *Guidelines for early childhood education programs in associate degree granting institutions* (position statement). Washington, DC: Author.

National Association for the Education of Young Children. (1994). Conceptual framework for early childhood professional development (position statement). *Young Children, 49*(3), 68–77. Washington, DC: Author.

National Association for the Education of Young Children. (2001). *NAEYC at 75: Reflections on the past, challenges for the future.* Washington, DC: Author.

National Child Care Information and Technical Assistance Center. (2007a). *State requirements for minimum preservice qualifications and annual ongoing training hours for child care center teachers and master teachers in 2007.* Fairfax, VA: Author.

National Child Care Information and Technical Assistance Center. (2007b). *State requirements for minimum preservice qualifications, and annual ongoing training hours for FCC home providers in 2007.* Fairfax, VA: Author.

National Child Care Information and Technical Assistance Center & National Association for Regulatory Administration. (2009). *The 2007 child care licensing study.* Lexington, KY: National Association for Regulatory Administration.

National Council for Accreditation of Teacher Education. *Experts investigate how to apply the science of child development in teacher preparation.* (n.d.). Retrieved April 1, 2009, from http://www.ncate.org/public/060208_FCD.asp.

Office of Head Start (2008). *Head Start program performance standards.* Program Design and Management, Subpart D, §1304.52, Human resources management, (b)(1). Washington, DC: Author.

Pennsylvania Administrative Code, Title 22, Education, Part I, State Board of Education, Subpart C, Higher Education, Chapter 49, Certification of Professional Personnel.

Regulations of Connecticut State Agencies, Title 19a, Public Health And Well-Being, Department of Public Health (5), Child Day Care Centers and Group Day Care Homes, Section 19a-79-4a, Staffing, (d)(2).

U.S. Department of Commerce, U.S. Census Bureau; and U.S. Department of Labor, Bureau of Labor Statistics. (2005). *Current population survey: Annual social and economic supplement, 2005.* Washington, DC: Authors.

U.S. Government Accountability Office. (2003). *Head Start: Increased percentage of teachers nationwide have required degrees, but better information on classroom teacher's qualifications needed.* Washington, DC: Author.

U.S. Office of Education. (1943). *Nursery schools vital to the war effort* (School Children and the War series). Washington, DC: Federal Security Agency.

U.S. Office of Special Education Programs. (2002). *Twenty-five years of progress in educating children with disabilities through IDEA.* Washington, DC: Author.

4

Early Childhood Competencies: Sitting on the Shelf or Guiding Professional Development?

Pamela J. Winton and Tracey West

In the early childhood field, the importance of a highly competent and confident workforce serving young children and families is undisputed. The role of professional competencies and professional development as essential components in a causal sequence that leads to positive outcomes for all children is also recognized. An area of lesser agreement is how to define and organize competencies and how to plan, deliver, and evaluate professional development which ensures that effective practices related to the competencies are implemented. Those responsible for early childhood professional development need to determine specifically which practitioners (*who*) need *what* knowledge, dispositions, and skills to bring about positive outcomes for children. They must determine *how* each individual should best be prepared and supported in order to acquire and implement specific practices to promote positive outcomes for children. They must also ensure that early childhood practitioners have access, resources, and support to participate in professional development. The alignment of *who*, *what*, and *how*, together with an infrastructure to support that alignment, is

key to ensuring that every young child has the advantage of being educated
and cared for by a competent and confident teacher (Buysse, Winton, &
Rous, 2009; National Professional Development Center on Inclusion,
2008). However, such alignment, while critical, is far from realization. The
purpose of this chapter is to examine the following topics:

- The state of the field in early childhood competencies and competency
  systems

- The state of the field in early childhood professional development systems

- Challenges, strategies, and recommendations for aligning competencies
  with professional development.

THE STATE OF EARLY CHILDHOOD COMPETENCIES AND COMPETENCY SYSTEMS

Defining Competencies

Competencies are commonly defined as what a person knows and can do:
the knowledge, skills, and dispositions necessary to function effectively in
a role (Center for the Study of Child Care Employment, 2008; Hyson,
2003; Winton, McCollum, & Catlett, 2008). They provide the foundational link in efforts to prepare effective teachers so that they in turn can
provide high-quality educational experiences to children. Once competencies are established and accepted, the infrastructure that supports the
acquisition of the core knowledge and skills set forth in the competencies
(a professional development system) and a system of accountability can be
put into place (Howes et al., 2008).

The terms *competencies, core knowledge,* and *personnel standards* are
often used interchangeably; however, differences between them exist.
The difference between competencies and core knowledge has been articulated by the National Child Care Information and Technical Assistance
Center (NCCIC), which defines competencies as the observable skills
teachers need to master and core knowledge as the central concepts that
teachers must know and understand (National Child Care Information
and Technical Assistance Center, 2007). Standards provide a set of expectations or benchmarks for measuring whether, and if so, at what level educators have mastered the core knowledge and skills; standards are
frequently used as a guide for accreditation or licensing and tend to
describe "the qualifications and credentials needed" to work in certain
roles (Harbin, Rous, & McLean, 2005, p. 142). For instance, a standards
framework might organize core knowledge and skills into levels according to job title or experience level (e.g., core competencies for teachers,

advanced competencies for administrators). In spite of these clear definitions found in the literature, the terms are used in somewhat confusing ways. National organizations have developed personnel standards that usually include competencies, whereas states have developed early childhood competencies that are organized within a standards format. It is unclear why states and national organizations do not use similar terminology in describing these efforts to define what practitioners should know and be able to do. In spite of the distinction between core knowledge and competencies in the literature (National Child Care Information and Technical Assistance Center, 2007), statements about knowledge and statements about skills usually are intermingled and their subject matter defined as competencies, organized within a standards framework. To complicate matters further, professional organizations and states have also developed standards focused on early childhood programs serving young children. In conversations about early childhood standards, confusion over the focus (e.g., programs to prepare adults or programs to serve young children) is frequent.

National Standards for Early Childhood Educators

Several national organizations have developed standards for early educators, chief among them are the National Association for the Education of Young Children (NAEYC), the Council for Exceptional Children/The Division for Early Childhood (CEC/DEC), the Council for Professional Recognition, and the National Board for Professional Teaching Standards (NBPTS). Standards developed by these major organizations share common characteristics. As already mentioned, standards usually are organized by level of experience or education (e.g., beginner, intermediate, advanced) and by content domain. Although terminology or titles for content domains differ, the topical foci are similar and generally include child development, relationships with families, assessment, teaching practices or methods, and professionalism.

Where these standards differ the most is in their target audience and purpose. Each set of standards targets a specific segment of early childhood. NAEYC standards are geared toward the early childhood workforce, DEC standards are for early childhood special educators and early interventionists, Child Development Associate (CDA) standards serve as the basis for a national credentialing program for early childhood practitioners without degrees, and NBPTS standards are used to credential licensed preschool teachers. The purpose of the standards varies by organization (e.g., certification, licensure). In all cases, use of the standards is voluntary. Moreover, it is possible to work as an early childhood teacher in certain settings without meeting any set of standards.

Preparing Early Childhood Professionals: NAEYC Standards for Programs   NAEYC has developed standards to provide guidance for higher education programs that prepare early childhood practitioners working with children from birth to 8 years (Hyson, 2003). NAEYC established five core standards that represent the common expectations for three levels of teaching: associate, initial licensure, and advanced. The core standards are identical for each level, but the depth and breadth of knowledge and skill increase from level to level. The standards for advanced programs include an additional focus on skills that are critical for leadership and on areas of specialization (e.g., master teacher, policy specialist, administrator). They also include an increased focus on preparing professionals to work with all children, including culturally diverse children and those with special needs. According to the NAEYC (2006) document *Where We Stand on Standards for Programs to Prepare Early Childhood Professionals*, the standards are based on research and professional values in the early childhood field. NAEYC provides a rubric for describing the progress of candidates within each level of standards.

Early Childhood Special Education/Early Intervention (Birth to Age 8) Professional Standards and Specialist Standards with CEC Common Core Content   CEC/DEC has developed standards designed to guide programs for institutions of higher education in the licensure of early childhood special education teachers and early intervention teachers working with children from birth to 8 years (Council for Exceptional Children, 2008; Division for Early Childhood, 2008). The standards are organized for two levels of educators: beginning special education teachers and advanced special educators. Both standards are based on CEC's common core standards for all special educators, with the addition of content specific to early childhood. Beginning early childhood special educator standards target programs preparing entry-level early childhood special education and early intervention teachers; advanced standards are designed for programs preparing professionals for a leadership role in either field. Rubrics for measuring competence are not provided.

The Child Development Associate Assessment System and Competency Standards   The Council for Professional Recognition has developed CDA competency standards (Council for Professional Recognition, 2006). The CDA is a national credentialing program designed primarily to meet the need for guidance in standards and professional development on the part of the large number of early childhood practitioners without degrees. The standards serve two purposes: They describe the skills needed by child care providers, and they provide a means of evaluating those skills (Council for Professional Recognition, 2006). The CDA is the most common minimum qualification for child care directors and master teachers (National Child Care Information and Technical Assistance Center and the National Association for Regulatory Administration, 2009). CDA competency standards are separated into six competency goals that are relevant to all early childhood settings (e.g., centers, family child care homes) serving children from birth to 5 years. Under each goal, functional areas provide examples, in the form of a checklist, of tasks or behaviors that help illustrate caregiver competence within that goal. The checklists are used as one part of the assessment process, which also includes portfolios, a questionnaire for parents, structured observations conducted by an advisor, and other forms of documentation.

National Board for Professional Teaching Standards Early Childhood Generalist Standards for Teachers of Children Ages 3–8

NBPTS has developed a set of eight standards for early childhood teachers: the Early Childhood Generalist Standards (NBPTS, 2001). These standards are based on the core standards that NBPTS utilizes for all teachers, with additional information specific to early childhood (ages 3–8). NBPTS standards provide a foundation for a voluntary certification process that may be undertaken by those licensed early childhood teachers with, at a minimum, a bachelor's degree. NBPTS certification is a rigorous process involving assessment and self-reflection, and is designed to recognize highly accomplished teachers. Teachers demonstrate their competency through performance-based assessment, including portfolios, videotapes, self-assessment, and more formal assessment activities. Assessment materials are submitted to a board for rating. Although the certification process is used to recognize and promote what accomplished prekindergarten teachers should know and be able to do, a 2007 NBPTS survey of schools, colleges, and departments of educations found that the majority of undergraduate and graduate teacher programs did not align their programs of study with NBPTS standards.

The existence of so many different sets of national standards reflects the complexity and ferment of the early childhood field and its history as a montage of early care and education programs supported by a market economy rather than a comprehensive public investment. An additional aspect of the fragmentation of the field is that children with disabilities historically have been educated in separate, specialized programs. That approach ended in 1975 with the passage of the Individuals with Disabilities Education Act (IDEA), which mandated the Education for All Handicapped Children Act (PL 94-142), which later became that young children with disabilities be educated in the least restrictive environment to the maximum extent possible. This history of fragmentation explains how the various standards came to be. With the increase in public investment in early childhood and the growing emphasis on teacher quality has come the expectation that regardless of differences in context and characteristics, all early childhood educators provide high-quality care and education to *each and every* young child. In this era of accountability and inclusion, the continuation of different sets of early educator standards is hard to justify.

Questions of interest related to the national standards include the following: To what extent are the different standards aligned across national organizations? Are competencies aligned with effective practices? Do competencies reflect the changing demographics of children and families being served by early childhood programs?

Alignment of Standards Across National Organizations

There have been some efforts by the major national organizations to address the need to align the different early childhood standards. For instance, NAEYC has worked with DEC to make sure that the standards provided by both organizations "complement and support one another" (Hyson, 2003, p. 17) so that all early childhood educators are prepared to work with children with and without disabilities. CDA competency standards are described as being aligned with NAEYC core standards (Hyson). The Early Childhood Generalist Standards set forth by NBPTS were designed to "reflect" NAEYC standards (Hyson, p. 145). The major professional organizations (DEC, NAEYC, and the Association for Teacher Educators) acknowledge that all early childhood educators should be prepared to work with children with and without disabilities and have expressed the need for a joint position on qualifications for all educators working with young children, including those with disabilities (Sandall, McLean, & Smith, 2000). These organizations are working toward consensus on a single set of standards and related competencies.

Alignment of Competencies with Practices

Competencies alone are not enough. The application of knowledge and skill to daily practices with children and families is where education happens. Both NAEYC and DEC have developed (separate) sets of practice guidelines and revised them on a regular basis: *DEC Recommended Practices in Early Intervention/Early Childhood Special Education* (Sandall, Hemmeter, Smith, & McLean, 2005) and *NAEYC Developmentally Appropriate Practice in Early Childhood Programs Serving Children from Birth Through Age 8* (Copple & Bredekamp, 2009). These two lists of specific practices, based on empirical and experiential knowledge, are designed to offer guidance to practitioners in making decisions about how to work most effectively with children and families (Snyder, 2006). Details about the processes used by the two organizations to develop and validate the guidelines are given on the NAEYC website (http://www.naeyc.org/dap/faq/chronology) and in Smith, McLean, Sandall, Snyder, and Ramsey (2005). Because the practices set forth in the lists are guidelines and not a set of operationally defined practices, neither organization has developed a set of rubrics, implementation checklists, or even tools for assessing the extent to which practitioners implement the practices. The conceptual link between practice guidelines and personnel standards within each organization is assumed to be strong and reflective of each organization's core values, mission, and knowledge base. However, as with the personnel standards, there has been no systematic alignment across the two sets of practice guidelines from the two national organizations.

The long-term emphasis on the importance of having a set of guidelines agreed upon and validated by the national organizations has been reinforced by the accountability movement in education. The movement has introduced the concept of evidence-based practice, with the expectation that early childhood teachers will know about and use such practice to meet the individual learning and socialization needs of each child. There has been some confusion about the meaning of evidence-based practice, and questions have been raised about the relationship between the DEC and NAEYC practice guidelines, on the one hand, and evidence-based practice, on the other (Snyder, 2006). Some have defined evidence-based practice narrowly, as a set of research-based practices with step-by-step procedures validated through a rigorous review process (Council for Exceptional Children, n.d.; Odom et al., 2005). Others have defined the term more broadly, as a decision-making process based on the best available research and integrated with other sources of knowledge (e.g., family and professional wisdom and values) (Buysse & Wesley, 2006). The focus on a decision-making process suggests that having a list of recommended practices is important, but may not be sufficient for making decisions. Instead, practitioners must look to the research evidence to find empirical support for the intervention practices they might use; beyond that, they must learn how to appraise and interpret research evidence and apply it to their work with individual children and families in local contexts. This notion raises questions about the DEC and NAEYC practice guidelines. Should those guidelines reflect the fact that some practices are more solidly supported by empirical research than others and have a validated set of procedures that should be included in the standards and competencies of the professional organizations and taught as part of professional development? Should personnel standards include the skills required for finding and appraising research and for integrating that research with other sources of knowledge in order to make a decision? If evidence-based practice does not become part of standards and practice guidelines, then these accountability components (the evidence-based practice movement and the national standards and practice guidelines) are unlikely to serve meaningful roles in shaping outcomes for children and families.

Alignment of Competencies with Changing Demographics

The alignment of competencies with changing demographics of the children and families being served by early childhood programs is another area of concern. Since 1990, the percentage of non-Caucasian children under 5 years grew from 26% to 45% percent (U.S. Census Bureau, 1990, 2005), with increasing numbers of children being dual-language learners (U.S. Census Bureau, 2008). In addition, regular early childhood programs are serving more children with disabilities than ever before (Data Accountability Center, n.d.). National survey data indicate that the majority of early childhood teacher preparation programs (approximately 60%) view preparing early childhood special educators and early interventionists as part of their primary mission, yet less than half of those (approximately 40%) say that they offer a required course on working with children with disabilities (Chang, Early, & Winton, 2005; Early & Winton, 2001). Given that early childhood teacher preparation programs are accredited by the National Council for Accreditation of Teacher Preparation (NCATE) on the basis of NAEYC standards rather than DEC standards, it is unlikely that content related to disabilities is infused into other required courses (e.g., curriculum, child development). Survey data also indicate that teachers are not likely to be prepared to serve children with linguistic diversity: only 14% of bachelor's degree programs offer a course on this topic (Maxwell, Lim, & Early, 2006). If DEC and NAEYC standards for professional preparation are emphasizing knowledge and skills for teaching diverse groups of children, it does not appear to have influenced course offerings in early childhood teacher education programs. The survey findings suggest that increased efforts should be made to ensure that standards and the programs they influence in institutions of higher education reflect the demographic changes in children and families being served in early childhood programs.

State Competencies for Early Educators

Because of the increasing emphasis on both high-quality teachers and accountability, states have begun to address the need to develop competencies for early educators. At least 80% of states have developed competencies and/or core knowledge elements for early childhood educators (National Child Care Information and Technical Assistance Center, 2007). Questions of interest related to the state competency development movement include the following: Do states use any of the sets of national standards as a basis for their state competencies? If they do, which ones do they use, and to what extent are the state competencies similar across states?

Alignment of State Competencies with National Standards

States utilize a variety of resources in the development of competencies. Among these resources are the competencies of other states and national standards. In documents that describe their development process, some states report drawing on NAEYC standards for personnel preparation (Chappel & Nye, 2007; Kentucky Partnership for Early Childhood Services, 2008; Mactavish & Mactavish, 2002; Career Development Initiative of New York State, 2001). In a review of state competencies, Bellm (2005) found that the broad topics covered by state competencies and national standards were similar. These similarities suggest that there might be some consistency among states in the content of competencies. However, states have not been consistent in the organization of those competencies (Center for the Study of Child Care Employment, 2008), using different terminology (e.g., core knowledge, core content, core competencies) to refer to their content and identifying different numbers of, and different, content domains. States have also organized the competencies into frameworks for standards in different ways. Some have grouped competencies into levels of expertise based on roles of teachers; others have described expertise on the basis of educational level or on experience (Center for the Study of Child Care Employment). The absence of an agreed-upon standard set of national competencies and standards to draw upon undoubtedly makes the work of states harder.

Recent research calls into question the information provided by states which indicates that their state competencies are based on standards of national organizations. In a review of state certification standards for early childhood special educators that was conducted through web-site reviews and telephone interviews, the majority of states reported that they used national standards as the basis for their state standards. However, an item-by-item content analysis of the state standards found little to no correlation with the national standards of NAEYC or CEC/DEC (Stayton et al., 2009). Only 22% of the states included in the study were found to have 80% or better correlation with national standards (Center to Inform Personnel Preparation Policy and Practice in Early Intervention and Preschool Education, 2008).

Alignment Between Competencies for Special Educators and General Educators

A small number of states have addressed the need to align general and special education standards by developing what is called "blended competencies," competencies that align content from the fields of general and special early childhood education. Blended competencies may be associated with blended certification programs developed by their state departments of education (Stayton et al., 2009). This movement began in the 1990s as a way of addressing the federal and state policy mandates for the inclusion of young children with disabilities in the least restrictive environment. There have been some attempts to study this policy initiative, but the absence of a consistent approach to defining and implementing blended certification has made that task difficult. In a national survey by Stayton and colleagues on early childhood state certification requirements, the researchers found three different certification models for integrating early childhood special education into the early childhood field among the seven states using blended certification. In addition, some of those states reported having multiple routes for certifying teachers to work with young children with disabilities.

Summary of Early Childhood Competencies and Competency Systems

In summarizing the state of early childhood competencies at national and state levels, the following conclusions can be drawn:

- Early childhood teachers work in a variety of settings and, depending upon the type of setting, are likely to have different requirements for levels of education and expectations of competency.

- Although many national early childhood organizations have developed standards and related competencies, these standards and competencies are not aligned across organizations.

- National standards and competencies are not necessarily aligned with evidence-based practice or demographic changes in the early childhood populations being served.

- National standards and competencies should guide state efforts to develop competencies, but evidence suggests that this cannot be assumed in any particular case.

- States are taking various approaches to developing state competencies, certification and licensure for early childhood teachers; thus, competencies, certification, and licensure vary from state to state.

- There are no agreed-upon tools or measures to assess teacher competencies or practices. Without these tools, it is difficult to determine whether professional development is accomplishing the goal of increasing effective teaching practices that lead to positive outcomes for children and families.

Given the preceding disparities, one must conclude that there is no one early childhood competency system. This conclusion is not surprising, in that there is no one early childhood system in general (Kagan, Kauerz, & Tarrant, 2007). It calls into question the role of competencies: Are they a driving force in professional development, or are they sitting on the shelf being used in a fragmented way or perhaps only at a superficial level (Winton, West, & Udell, 2009)? Our observation in working with states through the National Professional Development Center on Inclusion (NPDCI) is that much time and effort goes into the development of state competencies, but for the reasons described here, they often do not play a meaningful role in promoting positive outcomes for children.

THE STATE OF EARLY CHILDHOOD PROFESSIONAL DEVELOPMENT SYSTEMS

Definition of Professional Development

Historically, different terms have been used to describe professional development. The term *education* (also known as *preservice education*) is often used to describe the preparation of personnel in degree-granting programs offered by institutions of higher education. The term *training* or *in-service* is frequently used to describe continuing education efforts for practitioners in the workforce. Other approaches to supporting professional growth, such as coaching, consultation, and mentoring, are sometimes called "relationship-based supports" for professional development. Operational definitions of these approaches have not been agreed upon and terms are often used interchangeably. The confusion over terminology and the absence of an agreed-upon definition of professional development have together been detrimental to efforts aimed at studying teacher quality and effective approaches to professional development (Maxwell, Feild, & Clifford, 2005).

In response to the need for a definition of professional development to assist states in developing cross-sector plans to support the inclusion of young children with disabilities, NPDCI developed the following definition: Professional development is "facilitated teaching and learning experiences that are transactional and designed to support the acquisition of professional knowledge, skills, and dispositions as well as the application of this knowledge in practice" (National Professional Development Center on Inclusion, 2008, p. 3). This definition is broad and encompasses the different types of professional development described herein (e.g., preservice, in-service, technical assistance, reflective supervision, communities of practice, and the relationship-based approaches; visit the NPDCI web site at http://community.fpg.unc.edu/discussions/wiki-pd-approaches for proposed definitions of different types of approaches to professional development within the broad definition).

The broad definition addresses the historic disconnect between, on the one hand, early childhood personnel preparation implemented by institutions of higher learning, and, on the other, technical assistance and continuing education for early educators implemented by a variety of state or local agencies and entities—a disconnect that has contributed to the fragmentation of professional development systems (Winton, 2000; Winton, McCollum, & Catlett, 1997, 2008). Without a shared definition of professional development and a shared set of competencies linked with effective practices, the often espoused desires for articulation between in-service training and college credits and the alignment of academic content with real-world experiences are thwarted. The NPDCI definition was designed to help those with state-level professional development responsibilities envision how the separate early childhood professional development efforts taking place in the field might be brought together in an integrated fashion under a common, all-encompassing term.

Frameworks for Describing Professional Development Systems

In an attempt to promote planning around early childhood professional development in states, different organizations and projects have developed frameworks for describing professional development systems:

- NCCIC has developed a simplified framework for professional development. Sometimes referred to as "the tree" because of the schematic illustrating it in the literature, the framework is composed of the following five components: funding (the roots of the tree); core knowledge (the trunk); and qualifications, credentials, and career pathways; access and outreach; and quality assurance (the three branches of the tree) (National Child Care Information and Technical Assistance Center, 2007). (For a depiction of the tree, visit the NCCIC web site at http://nccic.acf.hhs.gov/pubs/goodstart/pd_section2b.html.)

- NAEYC has developed a policy blueprint to help states plan for early childhood professional development systems. The blueprint is sometimes called "the house" because of the schematic illustrating the planning framework. The base of the house consists of five policy-making principles: integration; quality assurance; diversity, inclusion, and access; and parity in compensation. The structure of the house is composed of six policy areas: career pathways, data, advisory structure, articulation, financing, and professional standards (LeMoine, 2008). (For a depiction of the house, visit the NAEYC web site at http://www.naeyc.org/policy/ecwsi#blueprint.)

- NPDCI developed a conceptual framework for planning cross-sector professional development as part of the organization's definition of the term. The central feature of the framework (the "inner circle") is the alignment of the following critical components: characteristics and contexts of the learners and of the children and families they serve (the "who"); what the learners should know and be able to do, defined as competencies, standards, and effective practices (the "what"); and the organizational and facilitation of learning experiences (the "how"). The outer circle of the framework consists of an infrastructure of supports (e.g., organizational structures, policies, resources, access and outreach) around the who, what, and how (National Professional Development Center on Inclusion, 2008). (For further information, visit the NPDCI web site at http://community.fpg.unc.edu/resources/articles/NPDCI-ProfessionalDevelopment-03-04-08.pdf/view.)

What these frameworks have in common is an appreciation of the complexity of professional development systems. They provide states with a means for considering the various components of the early childhood system that must be in place and properly aligned in order to promote effective teaching practices. For the most part, the NAEYC and NCCIC frameworks and supporting documents and tools focus more heavily on infrastructure issues (e.g., access, credentials, and articulation or transfer of college credits from 2- to 4-year institutions of higher learning) than they do on what teachers should know and actually do in practice settings and the professional development quality and methods that support effective teaching. The attention to infrastructure is critical because it reflects the decade-long emphasis on getting early childhood teachers into degree-granting programs, on the basis of research that showed a strong link between teachers having degrees and high-quality programs and child outcomes (Cost, Quality, and Child Outcomes Study Team, 1995). Recent reanalyses of data from several large-scale studies have called into question the strength of the relationship between having a degree, on the one hand, and better teaching and outcomes for children, on the other (Early et al., 2006, 2007). This reassessment has drawn attention to the need to examine the quality of professional development and to assess more carefully what approaches to it are effective with whom, on what topics, and under what circumstances. The desire to focus intensely on the quality of the implementation is one of the driving forces behind the NPDCI conceptual framework for professional development. Unfortunately, there is little rigorous research on the effectiveness of different approaches to professional development, in part because of the absence of agreed-upon definitions, implementation procedures, and assessment tools (Winton, 2006).

State and National Efforts to Achieve Cross-Sector Professional Development Planning and Implementation

Public investment in early childhood has raised awareness of the fragmentation and lack of attention to the quality of professional development. Recent policy initiatives are designed to address these challenges. For instance, the reauthorized Higher Education Opportunity Act (PL 110-315) establishes state grants to form cross-sector councils to develop early childhood professional development and career systems. The federal government's Early Learning Challenge Fund will provide grants to states to develop high-quality early learning systems for children from birth through age 5 and includes a focus on comprehensive professional development. Federal agencies have also funded a number of programs, including the following, to promote cross-sector early childhood professional development systems:

- The Natural Allies Project (2001–2006), funded by U.S. Department of Education, Office of Special Education Programs, worked with states to enhance personnel preparation programs by increasing the capability of community college and university faculty, state administrators, and family leaders to collaborate in preparing and supporting practitioners to work in inclusive settings. Findings from Natural Allies indicated that the model of collaboration to create systems change was successful (Winton & Catlett, 2009). In-state linkages between early childhood disciplines and sectors (e.g., early childhood education and early childhood special education) were strengthened, the ability of personnel preparation programs to support inclusion was enhanced, and the skills and knowledge of professional development providers related to inclusion were improved. Among the lessons learned were that a great amount of time and effort is necessary to foster cross-sector collaboration, that the faculty has to be willing to participate in state-level efforts (they were), and that it is important to have an individual in charge of planning and supporting collaboration. (For more information, visit the Natural Allies web site at http://www.fpg.unc.edu/~scpp/.)

- The NPDCI (2006–2011) is a current Office of Special Education Programs–funded project which works with states to ensure that early childhood teachers are prepared to educate and care for young children with disabilities in settings in which they are together with their peers without disabilities. NPDCI facilitates and supports collaboration among cross-sector early childhood leaders to develop a statewide cross-sector system of professional development related to inclusion. The members of the cross-sector groups include child care, public school (Title 1, pre-K, 619), Head Start, health or mental health, Part C, Institutions of Higher

Education, and family advocates. (For more information, visit the Early Childhood Community web site at http://community.fpg.unc.edu/.)

- SpecialQuest Birth–Five (2007–2010) is a current Office of Head Start–funded project that focuses on inclusion for children with disabilities, particularly children in Head Start and Early Head Start programs. SpecialQuest supports inclusion through embedding the project's approach, materials, and resources into professional development systems in states and local communities. Although SpecialQuest's emphasis is Head Start, it also includes other state and local agencies, such as Child Care, Early Intervention/Part C, and Early Childhood Special Education/619, as well as family support and other related programs, in the project's efforts. (For more information, visit the SpecialQuest Birth–Five web site at http://www.specialquest.org/.)

Summary of Early Childhood Professional Development Systems

Some promising approaches to helping states achieve cross-sector professional development plans are being described and discussed, but very few states have achieved a cross-sector professional development system. Most states have many different initiatives that at best, might be described as loosely coupled; most often they are disconnected from one another. One must conclude that in most states there is no comprehensive system that includes all of the relevant organizations, institutions, and entities that provide professional development to early childhood educators.

THE ALIGNMENT BETWEEN COMPETENCIES AND PROFESSIONAL DEVELOPMENT

A link between competencies (who needs to know and be able to do what) and professional development (facilitated teaching and learning experiences for acquiring and applying knowledge and skill) is essential. Given that neither early childhood competency systems nor professional development systems have been developed at national or state levels, how can any linkages be promoted?

A starting point in addressing this question is to identify state and national quality assurance initiatives that address teacher quality and to examine the relatively few linkages between competencies and professional development that do exist and could be promoted or strengthened within those structures. The quality initiatives addressed in the next section include 1) national systems for accrediting 2- and 4-year early childhood programs in institutions of higher education, 2) national systems for accrediting early childhood programs serving children, 3) state systems for licensing early childhood programs serving children, 4) state teacher certification and licensure programs, and 5) quality rating and improvement systems (QRISs) for early childhood programs.

Accreditation of 4-Year Early Childhood Programs in Institutions of Higher Education

NCATE is a voluntary quality assurance program widely used by undergraduate and graduate degree-granting teacher education programs in institutions of higher education across the country. Teacher education programs must demonstrate how NCATE standards are being taught in coursework and practicum settings. The NCATE standards for early childhood teacher education programs are linked to NAEYC's Standards for initial licensure and advanced and associate's degrees; the standards for early childhood special education and early intervention programs are linked to CEC/DEC Content Standards. The fact that a majority of early childhood teacher preparation programs identify preparing early childhood special education and early intervention practitioners as part of their primary mission without a need to demonstrate a link to DEC standards to NCATE is an obvious problem and could explain why coursework for working with children with disabilities is lacking in many of these programs (Early & Winton, 2001; Chang et al., 2005). NCATE does provide some recognition of blended early childhood teacher education programs in institutions of higher education. The guidance from NCATE to programs taking this route is limited to a short statement that blended programs must address both NAEYC and DEC standards in their programs of study. NCATE provides no guidance on how to integrate the two sets of standards, leaving that up to each program's discretion.

Accreditation of Two-Year Early Childhood Programs in Institutions of Higher Education

NAEYC launched a voluntary accreditation program for early childhood associate's degree programs in institutions of higher education in 2006 (For more information, visit the NAEYC website at http://www. naeyc.org/accreditation.) The program not only promotes the alignment of NAEYC standards with preparation for early educators in 2-year degree-granting programs, but also helps promote the articulation or transfer of credits from 2-year to 4-year degree-granting institutions of higher education. These goals provide continuity in the scope and sequence of learning experiences for early educators on the basis of a set of national standards. This is an important initiative with a potential impact on many teachers, since most early childhood teachers with degrees receive them from 2-year colleges and universities (Early & Winton, 2001). Again, the absence of a link to DEC standards is a problem, given the increase in numbers of young children with disabilities being served in general early childhood programs.

Certification or Licensure of Teachers

State departments of education are responsible for licensing teachers, including those early educators working in public prekindergarten settings. Certification requirements usually include the age range for which the individual is being certified, standards that the individual being certified must demonstrate, and assessments for documenting that standards have been achieved. Although DEC and NAEYC have recommended that a freestanding uniform certificate be developed for educators working with children from birth through age 8 years and adopted by states to ensure more congruence across states, that has not happened. Certification requirements vary greatly from state to state in regard to age range, standards, assessment methods, and models for integrating early childhood and early childhood special education certification (Stayton et al., 2009). The path for obtaining certification or licensure is usually through a state-approved early childhood bachelor's degree teacher preparation program. This means that alignment with national standards is possible if the teacher preparation programs are NCATE accredited. According to a recent report, 49 states and the District of Columbia have developed partnerships with NCATE (Stayton et al.), which suggests that most teacher preparation programs are reviewed on the basis of national standards for either early childhood (NAEYC) or early childhood special education (DEC), but not both (unless they are one of the small number of blended programs).

Licensure of Early Childhood Programs Serving Children

The child care regulatory agency in each state has the responsibility for issuing licenses to early care and education programs. Licensing is voluntary for child care programs; however, most states have strong public awareness campaigns to inform consumers of the importance of licensed care, and these campaigns have served to increase the number of licensed child care programs across the country. The emphasis in the licensure standards is on ensuring the basic health and safety of the young children being served by the programs. A few states have training requirements for continuing education for early educators (National Association of Child Care Resource & Referral Agencies, 2007). However, there is seldom any requirement for a level of education beyond high school. In addition, the training requirements are not often linked to state competencies or any kind of logical sequence of learning activities. The fact of the matter is that in its current form, the child care licensing program is not strongly linked to competencies and professional development and does not significantly aid early educators in becoming competent to serve all children, including those with disabilities.

Accreditation of Early Childhood Programs

NAEYC sponsors a rigorous voluntary accreditation system for early care and education programs for children from birth to kindergarten. The organization's purpose in establishing a national accreditation system was to improve the quality of child care programs beyond what is offered by the basic child care licensing programs implemented by states. Since the inception of NAEYC's system in 1985, more than 10,000 programs have been accredited. The system was revised in 2006 and is currently based on meeting 10 standards of high-quality programs: positive relationships among children and adults, curriculum, teaching, assessment of child progress, children's health, teachers, families, community relationships, physical environment, and leadership and management. The content within the program standards is similar to content within the NAEYC standards for professionals; however, the accreditation system and NAEYC's standards for programs are not formally linked or aligned. In addition, the accreditation system does not link to DEC personnel standards. This means that the criteria set forth may not be sufficient for meeting the needs of the large number of young children with disabilities being served in regular early childhood settings.

Quality Rating and Improvement Systems

QRISs are voluntary systems developed by states to assess and improve the quality of early childhood programs. Approximately 19 states have developed such systems, and many more are in the process of doing so (National Professional Development Center on Inclusion, 2009). Because there is no federal policy to guide the development of QRISs, there is variability across states in initiatives. Most QRISs include five components (NCCIC, 2007): quality standards, accountability, program and practitioner outreach and support, financial incentives for meeting standards, and consumer education (National Child Care Information and Technical Assistance Center, 2007). Two of these—quality standards and practitioner support—provide the strongest potential links between QRISs and professional development. Several states offer on-site technical assistance as a form of professional development to enhance program quality as part of their QRISs. However, these efforts are inconsistent from state to state, with no clearly defined procedures guiding the nature of the technical assistance or the way it is implemented. A link between the technical assistance and national or state competencies is unlikely. Instead, when education and training requirements for early educators are part of QRISs, they tend to rely on credentialing linked to clock hours of professional development or numbers of credit hours or courses. A review of state QRISs found few *apparent* requirements that the content of professional development be linked to competencies (Howes et al., 2008). There is also lack of consistent attention to how any components of such systems can support programs that include children with disabilities (Buysse & Hollingsworth, 2009; National Child Care Information and Technical Assistance Center, 2009; National Professional Development Center on Inclusion).

In sum, the potential link between a comprehensive set of competencies and professional development that one might expect to find in a number of different quality initiatives (e.g., licensing, certification, accreditation, QRISs) has not yet been realized.

CHALLENGES AND STRATEGIES FOR ALIGNING COMPETENCIES AND PROFESSIONAL DEVELOPMENT

A number of challenges remain to be addressed in attempting to align competencies and professional development:

- The absence of agreed-upon definitions and consistent usage of terms such as *competencies, standards*, and *professional development*, and the absence of agreed-upon approaches to professional development across national organizations, early childhood sectors, disciplines, and states

- The absence of an agreed-upon set of early childhood core competencies across organizations, institutions, sectors, and disciplines

- The absence of a uniform and distinctive early childhood certification for early educators

- Weak or nonexistent linkages among state competencies, professional development, and quality initiatives

- Little rigorous research on effective approaches for delivering professional development

- Few, if any, models of an early childhood cross-sector professional development system.

On the basis of these challenges and information in this chapter, we offer the following recommendations:

1. Agencies and institutions responsible for professional development need to agree on how to define and organize competencies for early educators. The competencies must be based on the best available research on effective practices and interventions for educating and caring for each child and must reflect the changing demographics of the children and families served in early childhood settings.

2. The competencies must be organized within a standards framework linked to a certification process that delineates the alignment between *who* needs to know and be able to do *what*. That framework needs to be linked with a description of *how* professional development should be delivered to achieve the level of impact (knowledge or skill) desired, a level that should match the practitioner's role and level of compensation and the professional development approach (e.g., workshops may be appropriate when the goal is awareness; on-site intensive coaching is appropriate for building skills).

3. Agencies and organizations need to agree on how to define professional development. They need to agree as well on conceptual frameworks, operational definitions, implementation procedures, and measurable outcomes for different approaches to professional development.

4. Mechanisms must be developed for conducting ongoing updates to competencies, standards, and professional development approaches in order to reflect emerging research findings and demographic changes.

5. Reliable and valid assessments of practitioners' knowledge and skills must be agreed upon so that an accountability system can be developed.

6. Competencies are needed for those providing professional development via different approaches. Reliable and valid assessments of the professional development providers' knowledge and skills must be developed.

7. Research on effective approaches to delivering professional development in accordance with evidence-based practices and on sustaining and scaling up the implementation of those practices is needed. The information gleaned from such research then needs to inform the various quality initiatives that have a professional development component.

National leadership and guidance must be provided to states to assist them in developing cross-sector early childhood professional development systems that align with national personnel standards, practice guidelines, competencies, and quality initiatives such as accreditation, licensing, and QRISs. Currently, there are many individual and disconnected efforts aimed at improving outcomes for children and families, sometimes occurring within the same agency and often being duplicated across the many entities that make up the early childhood field. A voice for unity and integration of federal and state efforts to ensure that each child has a highly competent, confident teacher must emerge from the two national professional organizations (NAEYC and DEC) and major federal agencies (U.S. Department of Health & Human Services and U.S. Department of Education) that shape policies and practices in the early childhood field today.

STUDY QUESTIONS

1. What are the differences among the terms *competencies, core knowledge,* and *personnel standards*?

2. Each set of standards targets a specific segment of early childhood. Which segments do NAEYC, DEC, CDA, and NBPTS standards target?

3. What are the five core standards and the three levels of teaching of the NAEYC standards?

4. What is the idea behind "blended competencies"?

REFERENCES

Bellm, D. (2005). *Establishing teacher competencies in early care and education: A review of current models and options for California.* Berkeley: University of California, Center for the Study of Child Care Employment. (ERIC Documentation Reproduction Service No. ED494181).

Buysse, V., & Hollingsworth, H.L. (2009). Program quality and early childhood inclusion: Recommendations for professional development. *Topics in Early Childhood Special Education, 29,* 119–128.

Buysse, V., & Wesley, P.W. (Eds.). (2006). *Evidence-based practice in the early childhood field.* Washington, DC: ZERO TO THREE.

Buysse, V., Winton, P.J., & Rous, B. (2009, February). Reaching consensus on a definition of professional development for the early childhood field. *Topics in Early Childhood Special Education, 28*(4), 235–243.

Career Development Initiative of New York State. (2001). *The New York State early care and education core body of knowledge framework: Essential areas of knowledge needed in working effectively with young children, birth through age 8* (2nd ed.). Retrieved August 14, 2009, from http://earlychildhood.org/pdfs/CoreBody.pdf

Center for the Study of Child Care Employment. (2008). *Early childhood educator competencies: A literature review of best practices, and a public input process on next steps for California.* Berkeley: University of California, Institute for Research on Labor and Employment, Center for the Study of Child Care Employment.

Center to Inform Personnel Preparation Policy and Practice in Early Intervention and Preschool Education. (2008). *Analysis of state certification requirements for early childhood special education data report.* Farmington: University of Connecticut Health Center, Author.

Chang, F., Early, D., & Winton, P. (2005). Early childhood teacher preparation in special education at 2- and 4-year institutions of higher education. *Journal of Early Intervention, 27,* 110–124.

Chappel, M., & Nye, S. (2007). *Nevada's core knowledge areas and core competencies for early care and education professionals.* Reno, NV: The Nevada Registry. Retrieved August 14, 2009, from http://www.nevadaregistry.com/forms/PDFs/CoreCompetencies10.15.07.pdf

Copple, C., & Bredekamp, S. (Eds.). (2009). *Developmentally appropriate practice in early childhood programs serving children from birth through age 8.* Washington, DC: National Association for the Education of Young Children.

Cost, Quality, and Child Outcomes Study Team. (1995). *Cost, quality, and child outcomes in child care centers public report.* Denver: University of Colorado, Economics Department.

Council for Exceptional Children, Division for Early Childhood. (2008). *Early childhood special education/early intervention (birth to age 8) specialist standards with CEC advanced common core.* Missoula, MT: Division for Early Childhood. Retrieved August 11, 2009, from http://www.dec-sped.org/uploads/docs/about_dec/position_concept_papers/DEC%20ECSE-EI%20w_CEC%20Advanced%20Standards%2010-08.pdf

Council for Exceptional Children, Division for Early Childhood. (n.d.). *Evidence-based practice—wanted, needed, and hard to get.* Missoula, MT: Division for Early Childhood. Retrieved August 14, 2009, from http://www.cec.sped.org/AM/PrinterTemplate.cfm?Section=CEC_Today1&TEMPLATE=/CM/ContentDisplay.cfm&CONTENTID=6515

Council for Professional Recognition. (2006). *The child development associate assessment system and competency standards.* Washington, DC: Author.

Data Accountability Center. (n.d.). *Individuals with disabilities education act (IDEA) data. Table 1-18: Children ages 3 through 5 served under IDEA, Part B, by disability category, race/ethnicity and state: Fall 2007.* Retrieved March 26, 2010, from https://www.ideadata.org/arc_toc9.asp#partbCC

Division for Early Childhood. (2008). *Early childhood special education/early intervention (birth to age 8) professional standards with CEC common core.* Missoula, MT: Author. Retrieved August 11, 2009, from http://www.dec-sped.org/uploads/docs/about_dec/position_concept_papers/CEC-DEC_Initial_Standards_10-08.pdf

Early, D.M., Bryant, D.M., Pianta, R.C., Clifford, R.M., Burchinal, M.R., Ritchie, S., et al. (2006). Are teachers' education, major, and credentials related to classroom quality and children's academic gains in pre-kindergarten? *Early Childhood Research Quarterly, 21*(2), 174–195.

Early D.M., Maxwell, K.L., Burchinal, M., Alva, S., Bender, R.H., Bryant, D., et al. (2007). Teachers' education, classroom quality, and young children's academic skills: Results from seven studies of preschool programs. *Child Development, 78*(2), 558–580.

Early, D.M., & Winton, P.J. (2001). Preparing the workforce: Early childhood teacher preparation at 2- and 4-year institutes of higher education. *Early Childhood Research Quarterly, 16,* 285–306.

Harbin, G., Rous, B., & McLean, M. (2005). Issues in designing state accountability systems. *Journal of Early Intervention, 27*(3), 137–164.

Howes, C., Pianta, R., Bryant, D., Hamre, B., Downer, J., & Soliday-Hong, S. (2008). *Ensuring effective teaching in early childhood education through linked professional development systems, quality rating systems and state competencies: The role of research in an evidence-driven system.* Charlottesville: University of Virginia, National Center for Research in Early Childhood Education.

Hyson, M. (Ed.). (2003). *Preparing early childhood professionals: NAEYC's standards for programs.* Washington, DC: National Association for the Education of Young Children.

Kagan, S.L., Kauerz, K., & Tarrant, K. (2007). *The early care and education teaching workforce at the fulcrum: An agenda for reform.* New York: Teachers College Press.

Kentucky Partnership for Early Childhood Services. (2008). *Overview of Kentucky's early childhood professional development framework.* Lexington: University of Kentucky, Human Development Institute, Author. Retrieved August 14, 2009, from http://www.education.ky.gov/NR/rdonlyres/7DABCC5F-F8BD-4290-B283-A868722BF2EA/0/RevisedPDFramework2008.pdf

LeMoine, S. (2008). *Workforce designs: A policy blueprint for state early childhood professional development systems.* Washington, DC: National Association for the Education of Young Children (NAEYC). Retrieved August 14, 2009, from NAEYC web site, http://www.naeyc.org/files/naeyc/file/policy/ecwsi/Workforce_Designs.pdf

Mactavish, M., & Mactavish, K. (2002). Common core content. In P. Turner (Ed.), *La Ristra: New Mexico's comprehensive professional development system in early care, education, and family support* (pp. 57–64). Santa Fe, NM: Children, Youth, and Families Department, Office of Child Development.

Maxwell, K.L., Feild, C.C., & Clifford, R.M. (2005). Defining and measuring professional development in early childhood research. In M. Zaslow & I. Martinez-Beck (Eds.), *Critical issues in early childhood professional development.* Baltimore: Paul H. Brookes Publishing Co.

Maxwell, K.L., Lim, C-I., & Early, D.M. (2006). *Early childhood teacher preparation programs in the United States: National Report.* Chapel Hill: The University of North Carolina, FPG Child Development Institute.

National Association for the Education of Young Children, (2006). *Where we stand on standards for programs to prepare early childhood professionals.* Washington, DC: Author. retrieved August 14, 2009, from http://www.naeyc.org/positionstatements/standards/ppp

National Association of Child Care Resource & Referral Agencies. (2007). *Threshold of licensed family child care (June 2007).* Arlington, VA: Author. Retrieved August 14, 2009, from http://www.naccrra.org/randd/licensing_training_qr/fcc_threshold.php

National Child Care Information and Technical Assistance Center. (2007). *Early childhood professional development systems toolkit.* Fairfax, VA: Author. Retrieved April 6, 2009, from http://nccic.acf.hhs.gov/pubs/goodstart/index.html

National Child Care Information and Technical Assistance Center and National Association for Regulatory Administration. (2009). *The 2007 child care licensing study.* Lexington, KY: National Association for Regulatory Administration. Retrieved August 18, 2009, from http://www.naralicensing.org/associations/4734/files/2007%20Licensing%20Study_full_report.pdf

National Professional Development Center on Inclusion. (2008). *What do we mean by professional development in the early childhood field?* Chapel Hill: The University of North Carolina, FPG Child Development Institute, Author.

National Professional Development Center on Inclusion. (2009). *Why program quality matters for early childhood inclusion: Recommendations for professional development*. Chapel Hill: The University of North Carolina, FPG Child Development Institute, Author.

Odom, S.L., Brantlinger, E., Gersten, R., Horner, R.H., Thompson, B., & Harris, K.R. (2005). Research in special education: Scientific methods and evidence-based practice. *Exceptional Children, 71*(2), 137–148.

Sandall, S., Hemmeter, M.L., Smith, B.J., & McLean, M.E. (2005). *DEC recommended practices: A comprehensive guide for practical application*. Longmont, CO: Sopris West.

Sandall, S., McLean, M E., & Smith, B.J. (2000). *DEC recommended practices in early intervention/early childhood special education*. Longmont, CO: Sopris West.

Smith, B.J., McLean, M.E., Sandall, S. E., Snyder, P., & Ramsey, A.B. (2005). DEC recommended practices: The procedures and evidence base used to establish them. In S. Sandall, M.L. Hemmeter, B.J. Smith, & M.E. McLean (Eds.), *DEC recommended practices: A comprehensive guide for practical application in early intervention/early childhood special education* (pp. 27–39). Longmont, CO: Sopris West.

Snyder, P. (2006). Best available research evidence: Impact on research in early childhood. In V. Buysse & P. W. Wesley (Eds.), *Evidence-based practice in the early childhood field* (pp. 35–70). Washington, DC: Zero To Three.

Stayton, V.D., Deitrich, S.L., Smith, B.J., Bruder, M.B., Mogro-Wilson, C., & Swigart, A. (2009). State certification requirements for early childhood special educators. *Infants & Young Children, 23*(1), 4–12.

U.S. Census Bureau. (1990). *U.S. Census 1990, 2005*. Retrieved August 12, 2009, from http://www.census.gov/

U.S. Census Bureau. (2008, September 23). One-in-five speak Spanish in four states: New Census Bureau data show how America lives. *U.S. Census Bureau News*. Retrieved August 11, 2009, from http://www.census.gov/Press-Release/www/releases/archives/american_community_survey_acs/012634.html

Winton, P. (2000). Early childhood intervention personnel preparation: Backward mapping for future planning. *Topics in Early Childhood Special Education, 20*(2), 87–94.

Winton, P. (2006). The evidence-based practice movement and its effect on knowledge utilization. In V. Buysse & P.W. Wesley (Eds.), *Evidence-based practice in the early childhood field* (pp. 71–115). Washington, DC: ZERO TO THREE.

Winton, P., & Catlett, C. (2009). Statewide efforts to enhance early childhood personnel preparation programs to support inclusion: Overview and lessons learned. *Infants and Young Children, 22*(1), 63–70.

Winton, P., McCollum, J., & Catlett, C. (Eds.). (1997). *Reforming personnel preparation in early intervention: Issues, models, and practical strategies*. Baltimore: Paul H. Brookes Publishing Co.

Winton, P.J., McCollum, J.A., & Catlett, C. (Eds.). (2008). *Practical approaches to early childhood professional development: Evidence, strategies and resources*. Washington, DC: ZERO TO THREE Press.

Winton P.J., West, T., & Udell, T. (2009, July). *Early childhood competencies: Sitting on the shelf or driving the system?* Paper presented at the 2009 Inclusion Institute, FPG Child Development Institute, Chapel Hill, NC.

II

Implementation at the State Level

5

What Do State Quality Rating Systems Say About Early Childhood Education Competencies and Professional Development?

Youngok Jung, Cathy Tsao, and Jennifer Vu

This chapter presents case studies that include quality rating systems (QRSs), professional development systems, and early childhood educator competencies. Professional development systems address qualifications and ongoing education and training for early childhood professionals; the scope of these systems can range from statements about the state's expectations for the talents of its early childhood work force, to more specific involvement in professional development registries, to approval of professional development content, to collaboration with institutions of higher education. Early childhood educator competencies describe the skills and knowledge that early childhood professionals are expected to have, and although the content of competencies can differ from state to state, there tends to be less variability in their form. Typically, they consist of a document that describes competencies in a number of domains and, sometimes, for staff at different levels. Other components of state early childhood systems might include early learning guidelines, program guidelines, child assessment, and program assessment. The degree to which the components of an early childhood system are aligned or explicitly linked varies from state to state and is often related to state priorities, the availability of resources, or the process (e.g., the sequence of development or the funding source or administrative home for each component) for developing the various components. For example, professional development systems may apply to all early childhood professionals within a state or only to those working in programs participating in the QRS. Similarly, in some cases early childhood educator competencies exist as a general resource for all early childhood professionals, whereas in other cases the QRS explicitly incorporates content from the early childhood educator competencies.

In this chapter, we use a case-study approach to examine the relationship among QRSs, professional development systems, and early childhood educator competencies in six states: Delaware, Kentucky, Maryland, New Mexico, Ohio, and Pennsylvania. (See Table 1.) We discuss this relationship from the perspective of the QRS; that is, we ask, What do the states' QRSs say about their respective professional development systems and early childhood educator competencies? We compare and contrast the qualifications that are required at each QRS level for various staff. Next, we examine professional development: the emphasis on preservice staff qualifications (education and training) or in-service ongoing professional development; the structure, content, and delivery of professional development; QRS infrastructure support for professional development; and incentives to facilitate staff participation in professional development. Finally, we describe links between QRSs and professional development systems on the one hand, and early childhood educator competencies on the other.

COMPARING QUALITY
RATING SYSTEMS ACROSS STATES

The relationship between QRSs and professional development systems varies widely with regard to 1) staff qualifications and the amount or type of professional development required at each level of the QRS, 2) the involvement of higher education systems, 3) the QRS's infrastructure support for professional development (e.g., whether it regulates trainer qualifications and whether it keeps professional development registries), and 4) links between the QRS and the professional development system, on the one hand, and early childhood educator competencies, on the other. However, across the six states examined, some broad generalizations do apply:

- In their staff qualifications, almost all six states require a postsecondary degree or the completion of an early childhood credential at higher levels of the QRS.

Table 1. Case study of quality rating systems, professional development systems, and early childhood educator competencies in six states

State		Early Childhood Component
Delaware	QRS:	Delaware Stars for Early Success (voluntary) Five levels; Star Level I meets licensing requirements Start date, 2007
	PDS:	Delaware First
Kentucky	QRS:	Kentucky STARS for KIDS NOW (voluntary) Four levels; all levels surpass licensing requirements Start date, 2001
	PDS:	KIDS NOW (Kentucky Invests in Developing Success)
	ECEC:	Kentucky Early Childhood Core Content
Maryland	QRS:	Early Childhood Accreditation Project (voluntary) Maryland Child Care Tiered Reimbursement Program (voluntary) Four levels; Level I meets licensing requirements Start date, 2001
	PDS:	Maryland Child Care Credentialing Program
	ECEC:	Maryland Model of School Readiness
New Mexico	QRS:	Look for the Stars (voluntary) Five levels; I star meets licensing requirements Start date, 2005
	PDS:	New Mexico Professional Development Initiative
	ECEC:	Common Core Content
Ohio	QRS:	Step Up to Quality (voluntary) Three levels; all levels surpass licensing requirements Start date, 2006
	PDS:	Career Pathways Model for Ohio Early Childhood & Afterschool Professionals
	ECEC:	Early Childhood Core Knowledge and Competencies
Pennsylvania	QRS:	Keystone STARS (voluntary) Four levels; all levels surpass licensing requirements Start date, 2002
	PDS:	Pennsylvania Keys to Professional Development
	ECEC:	Pennsylvania Core Body of Knowledge

Key: ECEC, early childhood educator competencies; PDS, professional development system; QRS, quality rating system.

- QRS standards generally require ongoing professional development, with different requirements based on the type of staff position (e.g, administrators/directors, classroom staff such as teachers and assistant teachers, or family child care providers).

- When QRSs differentiate between center-based care and other types
  of care, such as family child care, center-based care generally has the
  most stringent set of staff qualification and ongoing professional development requirements.

- All six states examined have some type of professional development
  system, which may include institutions of higher education, state and
  regional resources, and licensure and certification systems (Howes
  et al., 2008)

Differentiating Between Types of Child Care Settings

Child care can take a myriad of forms in a number of settings, including
center-based care; family child care; day camps; after-school programs,
care given by a relative or neighbor; and nanny care, either inside or outside
the home. Child care can be publicly funded, privately funded, or both.
Some of these settings are regulated by the state and require a license to
operate, whereas others (e.g., license-exempt care by relatives or friends)
are not thus regulated. However, only a limited number of child care settings are eligible to participate in the QRSs of the states examined in this
chapter: center-based care and both certified and licensed family child care,
depending on the state. Center-based care is generally defined as care provided in a state-licensed facility, professionally staffed by adults with training in child development and early childhood education and serving at least
four children in any range of ages from infancy to school age. Although
centers can vary in size, state licensing regulations generally specify a maximum adult-to-child ratio, which is typically lower for infants and toddlers
than for preschool or school-age children. Center-based care may include
publicly or privately funded programs such as Early Head Start and Head
Start, independent programs, state-funded preschool and prekindergarten
programs, campus-based programs, nursery schools, and programs affiliated with religious institutions. Family child care takes place in the home of
the provider (also referred to as the *owner-operator* or *primary caregiver*) and
may be staffed by one or more caregivers in addition to the provider. State
licensing regulations specify a maximum group size and adult-to-child
ratio. Family child care programs can serve children from infancy through
school age and often utilize mixed age groups; however, licensing requirements tend to limit the number of infants that can be enrolled at any given
time. Family child care may include private programs as well as those which
receive public funds.

   In addition to offering center-based care, Delaware includes two
different types of family child care in its QRS: large family child care and
Level II family child care, both of whose providers must be licensed by
the state. Large family child care in Delaware is defined as programs

serving 7–12 children of preschool age and younger in a home setting, while Level II family child care programs are allowed to care for up to 6 children of preschool age and younger and up to 3 school-age children. Kentucky's QRS includes Type I licensed child care centers (serving 4 or more children) and Type II certified family child care homes (serving up to 12 children). Maryland includes both center-based care and family child care homes in its QRS. Family child care homes in Maryland are defined as child care programs operated in private residences serving no more than 8 children at any given time. New Mexico includes both licensed child care centers and licensed family child care homes, the latter of which can take two forms: small family child care homes and large/group family child care homes. Although both take place in the provider's home, small family child care homes serve no fewer than 5, but no more than 6, children, whereas large/group family child care homes serve 7–12 children.

In addition to offering center-based care, Ohio includes in its QRS state-licensed home care known as Type A Homes, which are defined as programs that serve 7–12 children (or 4–12 children if 4 children are under 2 years of age) in the provider's personal residence.

Pennsylvania's QRS includes center-based care, group home care, and family home care. Group home care, which is certified by the state, is defined as care provided in a setting that serves between 7 and 12 children. Family home care, which is registered with the state, is defined as care given in a setting that serves 4–6 children and is staffed by 1 caregiver.

Generally, the requirements that apply to staff qualifications and ongoing professional development are more stringent for center-based programs than for family child care homes at corresponding levels of the QRS. For example, in Pennsylvania, the highest level of the QRS requires 1) all lead teachers and group supervisors to be at Level V or above on the career lattice (corresponding to an associate's degree or an associate-of-applied-science degree with 60 to 65 credits, 18 of which must be early childhood education credits), 2) 25% of teachers and group supervisors to be at level VI or above (corresponding to a bachelor's degree, including 30 early childhood education credits), and 3) all teachers to have 24 annual clock hours of professional development and to be involved in 2 professional growth and development activities annually. Directors at the highest level of the QRS are required to be at level VI or above on the career lattice, have 27 annual clock hours of professional development, and participate in 3 professional growth and development activities annually. However, for group home care, the highest level requires the primary staff person or operator to have a Child Development Associate or Child Care Professional credential, an associate's degree in early childhood education or 30 college credit hours in early childhood education or a related human services field, and 18 annual clock hours of training. For family home care, the highest QRS level requires the owner–operator, who is also the primary caregiver, to have a current Child Development Associate or Child Care Professional credential or 9 college credits in early childhood education or child development or a related field, and 18 annual clock hours of training.

In Delaware, the highest QRS level requires early childhood administrators to have completed a bachelor-of-arts or bachelor-of-science in early childhood education or a related field, to have earned the state Director Certificate or its equivalent, and to belong to a professional organization. In addition, at least half of all teachers are required to have completed an associates degree or 60 college credits in a bachelor's degree program in early childhood education or a related field. Those teachers who do not meet this requirement are required to have completed 9 college credits in early childhood education. For large family child care providers, the highest QRS level requires them to complete 12 college credits in early childhood education, business, or a related field, while family child care providers are required to have completed 9 college credits in early childhood education, business, or a related field. Finally, at the highest QRS level, both large family child care providers and family child care providers are required to belong to a professional organization.

Quality Rating System Levels and Staff Qualifications

In this section, we first discuss how states organize their QRSs at the broad systemic level and then look at the different requirements for staff qualifications. Since QRSs are generally aimed at increasing the quality of child care beyond basic licensing standards, the discussion will focus on expectations for programs striving for higher levels of quality.

Because Ohio has a different structure from that of the other five states, it is not included in the discussion but is covered in its own section.

Staff Addressed by Quality Rating Systems

Although terminology differs, there is a fair degree of consistency with regard to the types of staff that are addressed by the QRSs among the six states examined. (See Table 2.) In most states, the system specifies requirements beyond those needed for basic licensing in order to advance through the levels. For example, Ohio's QRS "uses licensing as a foundation" and "has three steps (levels) above Ohio's licensing standards" (Step Up to Quality Guidance Document, 2009, p. 8), while

Table 2.   Staff addressed by quality rating systems

State	Staff
Delaware	Early childhood administrators
	Early childhood curriculum coordinators
	Early childhood teachers
	Early childhood assistant teachers
	Large family child care license/provider
	Large family child care assistant
	Family child care licensee
	Substitute
Kentucky	Directors
	Staff
Maryland	Administrators (includes child care center directors and family child care providers)
	Staff (includes group leaders, assistant group leaders, and aides)
	Volunteers
	Substitutes
New Mexico	Staff who work directly with children
Ohio	Administrators
	Lead teachers
	Assistant teachers
Pennsylvania	Directors
	Staff (in child care and school-age care, includes aides, family child care providers, assistant teachers, assistant group supervisors, lead teachers, and lead group supervisors; in Early Head Start/Head Start, includes assistant teachers, aides, teachers, home visitors, and coordinators)

New Mexico integrated its system into its child care licensing regulations such that all licensed programs are required to comply with Level 1 criteria; participation at higher levels (up to Level 5) is voluntary and indicates compliance with standards of quality that surpass basic licensing regulations. All states include both administrators or directors (which may include curriculum coordinators), on the one hand, and classroom staff (including teachers, lead teachers, and assistant teachers), on the other, in their systems, and some states include family child care providers as well. Administrators and directors are responsible for the management and supervision of day-to-day operations in center-based programs; in Delaware, New Mexico, and Pennsylvania, this category explicitly includes curriculum coordinators who are responsible for the planning of instructional environments and activities. Classroom staff work directly with children in center-based settings and include lead teachers in all six states, as well as assistant teachers in Delaware, Pennsylvania, and Ohio, and aides in Pennsylvania and Maryland. Kentucky and New Mexico refer to the general categories of "staff" and "staff/caregivers," respectively, without further specification. Family or group home child care is typically staffed by an owner–operator (sometimes referred to as a *provider* or *primary caregiver*) and, in some cases, additional staff who work directly with children. There is variation both in the types of family child care staff that are addressed by the six QRSs and in the terminology that is used. The owner–operator and primary caregiver is included in all six states, in addition to teachers and assistant teachers in Ohio; aides in Pennsylvania; substitutes and assistants in Delaware, Kentucky, and Pennsylvania; and *staff* or *staff/caregivers* (without further specification) in Delaware, Kentucky, Pennsylvania, and New Mexico.

No state explicitly includes support staff working in areas such as food service, transportation, or administrative support, although some states used the broad category *all staff* without further elaboration. Maryland's QRS standards document specifically addresses the training of volunteers and substitutes, while, in contrast, Delaware intentionally excludes early childhood caregivers and interns from its standards because it "expects programs to move toward reducing the number of staff designated and qualified at these levels" (Family and Work Place, 2009).

Formal Education Requirements for Teachers

In all six states, programs at the first QRS level are required to have teachers who meet basic state licensing requirements. Then, in order to be rated at higher levels, programs are required to have teachers accumulate a number of college credits or clock hours in early childhood education or a related field and/or acquire credentials (e.g., director's credential), certifications (e.g., principals' certification), or higher degrees. In Pennsylvania, an associate's or higher degree is needed at higher levels for all or a proportion of teachers (e.g., for at least half of the teachers or group supervisors in a center-based program at Pennsylvania's second level; there is no similar requirement for family child care or group home care). At the highest QRS level in Delaware, half of the teachers in a center-based program need either an associate's degree or 60 college credits from a bachelor's degree–granting program in early childhood education or a related field. None of the six QRSs mandates a 4-year college degree, although in Kentucky teachers can use an associate's degree or higher to substitute for annual training hours starting with the second level.

Maryland differs from the other states in that the teacher qualifications specified by its QRS refer directly to its voluntary professional development system: the Maryland Child Care Credential, "which recognizes child care providers who go beyond the requirements of [s]tate licensing and registration regulations (Maryland State Department of Education, 2009)." The credential consists of six teacher levels and four administrator levels that reflect hours of training, years of work experience, and professional activities. The Maryland QRS then specifies that 60% of a program's lead teachers need to meet particular criteria set forth in the Maryland Child Care Credential in order for the program to achieve higher levels in the system. For instance, in order to reach the second level in the QRS, each family child care provider and 60% of lead staff in center-based care need to have a Maryland Child Care Credential at level 2 or higher. For ease of discourse, when referring to Maryland, the remainder of this chapter will discuss what is needed in the Maryland Child Care Credential up to the fourth level for this 60% of lead staff, since higher levels of credentials are above and beyond the minimum required by the QRS.

Formal Education Requirements for Administrators

As with teacher qualifications, at the first QRS level, all states require their programs to have administrators who meet basic state licensing requirements. An associate's degree is required at Level 3 for center-based administrators in Maryland and Pennsylvania (the second-highest level in both cases) and at the highest level for group-home administrators in Pennsylvania. (Family child care programs in Pennsylvania do not require an associate's degree.)

Center-based programs in Maryland and Pennsylvania require administrators to have a bachelor's degree only at the highest QRS level, but there is no bachelor's degree requirement for administrators in Pennsylvania's group home or family child care programs, even at the highest levels. The highest level of Delaware's system requires administrators in center-based settings to have a bachelor's degree and the Delaware Director Certificate, although curriculum coordinators need to only have a bachelor's degree. Delaware requires family child care providers at level "Three Stars" and beyond to have college credits in early childhood education, in business, or in a field related to early childhood education. In no states is a master's degree (or higher) required, although it is mentioned at higher levels for administrators in Maryland and Pennsylvania

As with teachers in Kentucky, administrators can use an associate's degree or higher to substitute for annual training hours, starting with the second QRS level, although in center-based care having either degree is not a requirement. In both licensed and certified family child care homes in Kentucky, directors can have either an associate's degree or a Child Development Associate credential.

Multiple Paths to Meeting Qualifications

As suggested in the formal education requirements for teachers and administrators summarized in the preceding two sections, some states accept alternatives to a postsecondary degree. For example, in Kentucky, programs can meet the staff qualification criteria at higher QRS levels if administrators, classroom staff, or family child care providers possess certain credentials in lieu of a college degree.

The Case of Ohio   Ohio differs from other states in that, rather than defining staff qualifications at each level of the QRS, a centralized point system called Career Pathways is used. Career Pathways integrates formal education (degree, credit hours, area of study), training, experience, and specialized credentials and certifications, and provides a way for early childhood professionals to document their professional accomplishments. It also serves as a mechanism by which the state of Ohio can both gather information about its early childhood workforce and support advancement within the system. Although all early childhood professionals are eligible to participate in the system, it was developed specifically to collect required information on staff employed in programs applying to be involved in the QRS pilot program. There are six early childhood professional levels in Career Pathways; administrators and staff can move up by accumulating points in the four areas of formal education, in-service training and continuing education, experience, and credentials and certifications (e.g., advancement to Level 3 requires 150 to 249 points). Since Career Pathways allows flexibility in how early childhood professionals accumulate the points needed at each level, there is no standard requirement for staff qualifications (education, experience, or a combination of both) at different levels of the QRS.

Each level of Ohio's QRS specifies qualifications for staff and administrators. The qualifications are described both in terms of Career Pathways levels and in terms of alternatives for meeting requirements [e.g., at Step 2, the administrator is required to have an associate's degree in early childhood education or to have advanced to Career Pathways Level 3, *and* 50% of lead teachers are required to have an associate's degree in early childhood education (or a related field for school-age teachers) or to have advanced to Career Pathways Level 3].

THE QUALITY RATING SYSTEM AND THE STRUCTURE, CONTENT, AND DELIVERY OF PROFESSIONAL DEVELOPMENT

Professional development is focused on supporting professional growth, increasing qualification levels, and improving staff knowledge and competencies related to children's learning and development. Traditionally, there has been a distinction between preservice and in-service professional development. However, these categories tend not to reflect the current realities of either early childhood workforce development or QRS support for it; for example, many community colleges require child development students to participate in fieldwork practicums and do not consider the work to be preservice, since the students are working in the early childhood field prior to receiving a college degree. Similarly, because QRSs are generally aimed at encouraging child care programs to achieve increasingly higher levels of quality, some of the QRSs in the six states examined provide support for activities that might traditionally have been considered preservice," such as staff pursuit of bachelor's degrees. The use of the term "in-service" may also be fading as the early childhood field tries to move away from the notion of short-term, decontextualized workshops or training in favor of more individually meaningful, ongoing professional development that is related to accepted values, goals, or principles, that build on an individual's strengths, and that address areas for improvement. Therefore, in this chapter, rather than making the distinction between preservice and in-service training, we will address and describe what the different QRSs outline in terms of the ongoing professional development (including staff qualifications, courses, training, experiences, and activities) needed to advance from level to level.

Amount of Professional Development or Number of Professional Activities

A certain number of hours of professional development (i.e., courses, training) are required annually for both staff and administrators in nearly all of the states studied. The sole exception is New Mexico, which has no written guidelines that specifically address professional development. For states that differentiate among settings, QRSs usually require staff and administrators from center-based programs to engage in more professional development than staff and administrators from other types of programs; the exception is Ohio, which requires the same amount of professional development for center-based programs and family child care homes.

Delaware, Maryland, and Pennsylvania all require both staff and administrators to participate in a certain number professional activities annually. Among qualifying professional activities are belonging to a child care professional organization at the local, state, or national level; being a mentor; and presenting at a conference. Increasing numbers of professional activities, which are counted on a yearly basis (and thus are not accumulated across a career) are required at higher levels of the QRS.

Content of Professional Development

The six states vary in the degree to which the QRS specifies professional development content. The variability ranges from a requirement to have a written professional development plan for each staff member (i.e., Delaware, Kentucky, New Mexico, and Pennsylvania), to a requirement of an annual number of professional development hours or activities (with or without recommendations or requirements regarding content (i.e., Pennsylvania and Kentucky), to a requirement that prerequisite or ongoing professional development activities address particular content and/or are approved in advance (i.e., Maryland and Ohio). Content specified across states may include, but is not limited to, training in the following areas: child development, observation and assessment, professionalism, nutrition and health issues, working with families, working with children with special needs, and curriculum planning. Similarly, the relationship between professional development requirements and accountability for their implementation varies, with some states requiring written professional development plans for each staff member, but no mandate to implement those plans. Further, those states which do specify professional development content vary with regard to the developmental, policy, or regulatory emphasis of that content. For example, Maryland describes professional development as an opportunity for early childhood professionals to learn about new developments in the field as well as improve individuals' credential levels. Delaware requires staff to be trained in the state's early learning guidelines, use of the environmental rating scales, and curriculum planning. Ohio has the most specific requirements in terms of both intensity and content, including prerequisites of 7.5 hours of "New Administrator Rules Review Training" for administrators, 20.5 hours of training in the state's "Infant/Toddler Early Learning Guidelines" lead and assistant teachers of infants or toddlers, and 10 hours in the state's "Early Learning Content Standards" for preschool lead and assistant teachers; only after completing these prerequisites can staff participate in other professional development activities, but those activities must be approved in advance by the QRS. Effective July 2010, all classroom, administrative, and family child care staff in New Mexico's system will be required to complete the 6-hour "Quality Early Childhood Programs for All" course (or its equivalent) on children with diverse abilities.

Only three states' QRSs mention curriculum planning for teachers and administrators. In Delaware, half of all lead teachers in center-based programs at Star Level 3 must receive training in curriculum planning; this requirement increases through Star Level 5 (the highest level), at which all lead teachers in a particular program are required to have training in curriculum planning. Administrators in Delaware's center-based and family child care programs at Star Level 3 are required to have training in more comprehensive curriculum planning. In Maryland, classroom staff from programs at the two highest QRS levels are required to have training in curriculum planning, a requirement that starts at the first level for administrators. At the second-highest level for child care centers in Pennsylvania, all teachers and assistant teachers are required to attend an annual professional development course on a number of subjects, one of which is curriculum planning. There are no requirements for administrators in Pennsylvania to receive training in curriculum planning.

Maryland's QRS is the only one that specifies work experience (for both staff and administrators). Higher levels require increasing years of experience working directly with children in an approved setting, with more work experience required overall for administrators than classroom staff. In addition, Maryland is the only state that requires administrators to have training in mentoring and coaching (at the highest level).

Both Delaware and Pennsylvania require some knowledge of the Early Childhood Environment Rating Scale, which can be achieved by receiving training. Delaware's requirement applies to administrators at the second-lowest QRS level, while Pennsylvania's requirement applies to administrators and classroom staff. Finally, both Kentucky and Pennsylvania require staff to have first-aid training.

Delivery of Professional Development

Professional development can be acquired in a number of ways, including taking college courses leading to credentials or degrees, attending conferences, through distance learning, and attending workshops or training. The acceptance of diverse delivery methods in a QRS is intended to facilitate participation in professional development.

In all six states examined, any state-approved community college and university course in child development and early childhood education accredited by the National Council for Accreditation of Teacher Education (NCATE), NAEYC's Early Childhood Associate Degree Accreditation, or the Council for Early Childhood Professional Recognition's Child Development Associate National Credentialing Program is counted toward professional development. In addition, college credits can be transferred from institution to institution and applied toward credentials and degrees, thereby facilitating the early childhood education staff's transition from one professional development level to another. Many 2-year and 4-year state colleges offer early childhood education or child development courses that are required to meet state standards for credentials and degrees required for a person to work in the early childhood education field. In particular, the majority of courses offered in the 2-year colleges are common core courses in child development and early childhood education that could be applied to earn credentials or degrees. The agreement in courses among institutions of higher education establishes a continuum of professional education and assists early childhood education staffs in improving their qualifications by earning credentials and degrees without any loss of credits.

QUALITY RATING SYSTEM INFRASTRUCTURE SUPPORT AND INCENTIVES

The QRSs in the six states examined exhibit similarities and differences in the kinds of infrastructure support for professional development and incentives for staff participation that they provide. Most commonly, these supports and incentives include required or recommended training offered either directly by the QRS or the professional development system or through institutions of higher education, community organizations, newsletters, or online calendars listing training opportunities, professional development registries, and scholarship, grant, or reimbursement programs.

Scholarship, grant, or reimbursement programs are intended to help programs move up the QRS levels and to improve staff compensation and retention. Scholarship programs are particularly important for professional development because they provide funding to early care and education staff to pay for the college courses specified in the QRS (Mitchell, 2005). Delaware, New Mexico, Ohio, and Pennsylvania offer Teacher Education and Compensation Helps (TEACH) Early Childhood Project scholarships, which provide financial support to staff pursuing state or national credentials or postsecondary degrees in early childhood education. Delaware and Ohio limit eligibility for their TEACH Early Childhood scholarships to staff working in programs that are participating in their QRSs, and Pennsylvania gives priority for new scholarship awards to staff working in programs that are participating in its system. New Mexico does not link eligibility to its system. Delaware restricts funds to helping a staff member meet the qualifications of his or her current QRS designation or to meet a specific system standard, while Ohio includes staff working in "emerging stars" programs (i.e., programs that do not yet qualify for the lowest level of the system). Of the six states examined, only Ohio provides a bonus or raise upon completion of the TEACH scholarship program, and that state, like others, requires scholarship recipients to commit to an additional period of employment (typically 6 months to 1 year) in the same program. Maryland offers tiered reimbursement and accreditation support to programs participating in its QRS, as well as training vouchers or reimbursement and a child care professional development fund through its child care credential program. Kentucky has an early childhood development scholarship that provides financial assistance for staff pursuing the Child Development Associate credential, an associate's or bachelor's degree in early childhood education, or the state's Early Childhood Development Director's Certificate.

Another support for professional development is a credential or certification program, although only half of the six states have such a program in place (beyond the Child Development Associate credential), none of those programs are tied exclusively to the QRS. There is some variability in the scope of the credential and certification programs. For instance, Delaware offers an online certificate for directors and a 60-hour course culminating in an infant/toddler certificate, while Kentucky and Pennsylvania have more comprehensive systems in place that include director and teacher credentials and certification, as well as more specialized programs leading to a trainer's credential (Kentucky), an interdisciplinary early childhood education certificate for early childhood professionals who have a bachelor's degree or higher (Kentucky), and early intervention qualifications and a certificate of competency (Pennsylvania).

Most states have incorporated existing career-ladder professional development standards into their professional development systems. The career ladder identifies professional preparation for each position and serves as a guideline for training, courses, experience, and education required for the next professional development level. Pennsylvania, Ohio, and New Mexico include the attainment of levels on career ladders as part of their QRS standards for professional development. For instance, although it varies in the percentage of staff with qualifications, Pennsylvania's system requires programs that qualify for the second to fourth star levels to have staff who have completed a Child Development Associate credential, a certified child care professional credential, or an associate's degree or higher in early care and education or some other human development area. Similarly, Maryland's system is based on the attainment of the state's child care credential. Kentucky has a three-level credential system for its workforce in early childhood education. Delaware has an education pathway that assists potential early childhood education staff in preparing for employment qualifications as early as when they are in high school and in matching college credits with QRS levels and professional development.

Some states also offer technical assistance, which is typically individualized and customized in the form of mentoring and coaching to satisfy individual programs' needs and concerns. For instance, technical assistance can aid programs with their participation in QRSs and ratings. Typically, technical assistance is offered through a regional center (e.g., in Kentucky, New Mexico, Ohio, and Pennsylvania) on a one-to-one basis or to a small group. However, technical assistance may not be accepted as professional development because it often does not have a set curriculum.

In Pennsylvania, technical assistance is closely aligned with the state's QRS and provides support to programs in meeting the system's standards and improving program quality. Through key regional staff and other agencies, technical assistance not only provides introductory information and education on Pennsylvania's QRS, but also assists programs in developing a site improvement plan to reach higher levels (e.g., a better environmental rating scale and enhanced professional development) in the system on the basis of system standards.

Several states have identified particular needs or opportunities in their communities and engage in additional efforts to facilitate staff participation in professional development. In order to "support the state's early care and education career development system" (Children and Families First), Delaware provides access to toys and other learning materials, laminators, copiers, and die-press systems through its resource center network and mobile resource vans. Ohio's network of infant and toddler specialists, early language and literacy specialists, and school-age specialists provides professional development support to teachers through the state's QRS. Pennsylvania has embarked on a number of professional development initiatives, including Mind in the Making, a multifaceted national communications initiative in learning created by the Families and Work Institute and New Screen Concepts; the Regional School-Age Child Care Projects, which provide professional development, technical assistance, and a resource-lending program to public and private after-school programs across the state; and the Infant Mental Health Project, a 2-year needs assessment, gap analysis, and pilot project aimed at promoting infant mental health through professional development and support for infant and toddler caregivers.

Regulation of Trainer Qualifications

In order to ensure the quality of professional development activities, most of the six states examined have established trainer and/or training approval systems (National Child Care Information and Technical Assistance Center). A trainer approval system defines qualifications that must be met by individuals who offer early childhood professional development, while a training approval system defines standards that training activities must meet (e.g., providing child development content and presenting principles of adult learning). For instance, Pennsylvania requires trainers to have at least a bachelor's degree, accumulate 30 credit hours in early childhood education, and be approved by the Pennsylvania Quality Assurance System. Pennsylvania's QRS, Keystone STARS requires that all professional development activities be approved by the system.

As a component of their professional development systems, some states, including Ohio and Pennsylvania, have a trainer registry, which is a record of trainers and their qualifications, or personal and training registries, which track participants' competed training, education, and professional activities. These registries are used to collect, track, acknowledge, and manage workforce data in the early childhood field (National Child Care Information and Technical Assistance Center). The data can then be used to analyze trends in participation in professional development, to evaluate individuals' or programs' achievement in moving up a career ladder or the levels of a QRS, and to attain credentials and accreditation.

Since November 2009, Delaware's early childhood professional development system has been coordinated and delivered by the new Delaware Institute for Excellence in Early Childhood, a partnership between the University of Delaware and Children & Families First. Of the six states studied, Delaware is the only one whose professional development system is formally managed by a university, although other states have developed partnerships between their systems and institutions of higher education.

Links Between Quality Rating and Professional Development Systems and Early Childhood Education Competencies

According to the National Child Care Information and Technical Assistance Center, early childhood education competencies, also labeled core knowledge and competencies, are linked to early learning standards, developmental theory, and developmentally appropriate practice, and describe the knowledge and skills necessary to work effectively with children, families, and other early childhood professionals. Early childhood education competencies can serve as a foundation for organizing, approving, and offering professional development courses and training, as well as defining levels of training and education on a career ladder (National Child Care Information and Technical Assistance Center). In addition, most states' competencies are used to provide a framework for professional growth and development and for financial rewards.

In general, early childhood education competencies consist of a rationale section, a core knowledge area, and different levels of essential competencies expected in each area. The rationale section emphasizes the importance of the area by showing relations between the area, child outcomes, and program quality. The core knowledge area describes a broad range of essential knowledge and concepts that all early childhood education staffs need to know and be able to do to facilitate young children's learning and development. The competencies describe a range of observable skills and behaviors that early childhood education staffs need to have at different professional levels. In addition, the levels of competencies are often coordinated with a state's career ladder system and assist early childhood education staffs in making transitions to the next professional level.

Topics addressed in early childhood education competencies tend to fall into the broad areas of child development, environment and curriculum, observation and assessment, classroom practices, leadership, and working with families, but there are idiosyncrasies as well. (See Table 3.) These topics correspond to the states' early learning guidelines that articulate expectations for development and learning in the early childhood years. In most states, early learning guidelines are aligned with the seven areas of the Head Start child outcome framework (language and

Table 3. State-by-state comparison of content of early childhood education competencies

Competency	DE	KY	MD	NM	OH	PA
Child development, growth, and learning	✓	✓	✓	✓	✓	✓
Communication						✓
Environment and curriculum	✓	✓		✓	✓	✓
Health, safety, and nutrition	✓	✓	✓	✓	✓	✓
Observation and assessment	✓	✓	✓	✓	✓	✓
Program administration and organization				✓		✓
Professionalism	✓	✓	✓	✓	✓	✓
Socioemotional development	✓					
Special needs			✓			
Working with families and/or the community	✓	✓	✓	✓	✓	✓
Specific competencies for administrators	✓			✓		✓
Specific competencies for family child care providers						✓
Specific competencies in family, infant, and toddler studies				✓		

literacy, math, science, the creative arts, health and nutrition, socioemotional development, and approaches to learning), the seven areas of National Association for the Education of Young Children (NAEYC) Standards for Early Childhood Professional Preparation (promoting child development and learning, building family and community relationships, observing, documenting, assessing to support young children and families, teaching and learning, and becoming a professional), and the 10 areas of the NAEYC accreditation standards (relationships, curriculum, teaching, assessment of child progress, health, teachers, families, community relationships, physical environment, and leadership and management).

All six states examined have developed early childhood education competencies with some variations in the content of core knowledge and in the levels of competency. Contents commonly included in at least most of the states are child development and growth; health, safety, and nutrition; observation and assessment; professionalism; working with families and/or communities; and environment and curriculum. Other contents included in some states' competencies are communication (Pennsylvania), program administration (Kentucky, Pennsylvania), socioemotional development (Delaware), and special needs (Maryland). Kentucky and Pennsylvania address program administration in their competencies, and Maryland includes a domain on caring for children with special needs in inclusive settings. In five of the states, excluding Maryland, competencies are classified into three to five different levels, with higher levels requiring more advanced skills. Kentucky classifies competencies into five different levels, Delaware into four, and the remaining three states (Kentucky, Ohio, and Pennsylvania) in three. Maryland is the only state that defines competencies in terms of the attainment of clock hours in professional development in each content area.

States' competencies are linked to the states' QRSs and professional development in various ways. Delaware and Pennsylvania are the only states whose QRS standards are explicitly linked to early childhood educator competencies; although the standards of the other four states do not specifically mention early childhood education competencies, there are links to the professional development systems in those states. Delaware's standards at the five-star level for center-based programs require administrators to have the Early Childhood Education Director Certificate based on the Delaware First Administrator Competencies, which address the areas of administration, operations, personnel, and fiscal policies and procedures. The two-star level for center-based and family child care programs requires teachers and assistant teachers to complete an annual self-assessment based on the Delaware First Core Knowledge and Competencies. Pennsylvania's QRS addresses early childhood education competencies, but only with regard to administrators, who, at the one-star level, are required to complete their professional development with respect to the state's Core Body of Knowledge/Professional Development Record for Early Childhood and School-Age Practitioners.

The remaining four states—Kentucky, Maryland, New Mexico, and Ohio—have integrated their early childhood education competencies into their professional development systems to different degrees. The five levels of competency in Kentucky's Early Childhood Core Content (revised 2004) are reflected in various professional development programs and activities, and Maryland's Core of Knowledge Chart specifies the number of hours of training required in each competency area in order to fulfill the requirements of the state's child care credential. Competency areas for Ohio and New Mexico are aligned with those states' career matrices; in addition, New Mexico's Common Core Content and Areas of Specialization forms the foundation for early childhood courses in all of the state's colleges and universities.

Most early childhood education competencies are directed at classroom staff (or unspecified staff), but three states (Delaware, New Mexico, and Pennsylvania) have defined separate (or additional) competencies for administrators, and one state (New Mexico) has defined separate (or additional) competencies for a specialization in family, infant, and toddler studies. Pennsylvania, has defined separate (or additional) competencies for family child care providers, while Delaware, specifies that its early childhood education competencies are for center-based practitioners.

CONCLUSION

QRSs are one component of a state's early childhood development system. The development and implementation of QRSs relative to other components of statewide early childhood systems, such as professional development systems or early learning guidelines, followed a different process and time line in each of the six states we have examined. In addition, the various components of a state's early childhood system may have different administrative homes, including universities, departments of education, and departments of children, youth, and families, and these differences may play a role in the level of integration among components of the early childhood systems within each state. Although the six states vary in the degree to which their QRSs are formally linked to their professional development systems and early childhood educator competencies, they all share the perspective that improving the quality of child care is related to improving the qualifications, education, and ongoing professional development of staff. Furthermore, five of the six states' QRSs recognize national accreditation programs, such as that administered by the NAEYC, that also acknowledge the role of professional development in continuous program improvement. Because all of the QRSs in the six cases studied were implemented since 2001 and are therefore fairly new, future examination may reveal evolving relationships among QRSs, professional development systems, and early childhood education and educator competencies as each state's early childhood system matures.

STUDY QUESTIONS

1. What are the common contents of early childhood educator competency and professional development systems?

2. What are the types of child care settings addressed in QRSs?

3. What are the roles of professional development systems and early childhood educator competencies in QRSs?

4. On the basis of 1) the types of staff positions and child care settings and 2) the levels of quality ratings, what are the differences in staff qualification and professional development requirements?

5. What are the elements of QRSs to support early childhood education staff's participation in professional development?

REFERENCES

Children and Families First. *The resource center network*. Retrieved from http://www.familyandworkplace.org/providers/provider.rcn.locations.asp

Family and Work Place (2009). *Delaware Stars for Early Success 2009*. Retrieved from https://www.familyandworkplace.org/DEStars/.../StarsCenterStandards.pdf

Howes, C., Pianta, R., Bryant, D., Hamre, B., Downer, J., & Soliday-Hong, S. (2008). *Ensuring effective teaching in early childhood education through linked professional development systems, quality rating systems and state competencies: The role of research in an evidence-driven system*. Paper presented at the meeting of the National Center for Research on Early Childhood Education 2008 Leadership Symposium, Arlington, VA.

Maryland State Department of Education (2009). *Maryland child care credential program*. Retrieved from http://www.marylandpublicschools.org/MSDE/divisions/child_care/credentials

Mitchell, A. (2005). *Stair steps to quality: A guide for states and communities developing quality rating systems for early care and education*. Fairfax, VA: United Way Success by 6.

National Child Care Information and Technical Assistance Center. *Core knowledge*. Fairfax, VA: Author. Retrieved April 6, 2009, from http://nccic.acf.hhs.gov/pubs/goodstart/pd_section4.html

Step Up to Quality guidance document. (2009, January 7). Columbus, OH: Department of Job and Family Services. Retrieved April 13, 2009, from http://jfs.ohio.gov/cdc/stepUpQuality.stm

6

Professional Development Systems for Early Childhood Educators within a State and Federal Policy Context

Sandra L. Soliday Hong, Terri Walters, and Tamar Mintz

Policy makers have largely ignored the vital role of professional development in providing high-quality early care and education. As a result, the pursuit of professional development has been the responsibility of individual teachers. Recent thinking about quality in early care and education has taken the spotlight away from materials and structural features of the care environment, which traditionally have been emphasized in policies regulating early care and education, and focused it on the importance of children's actual experiences and the instruction they receive (Howes et al., 2008; Mashburn et al., 2008). These studies suggest that the experiences adults provide for children in their care have a greater long-term bearing on the children's development than do structural features of quality, such as the materials provided, the arrangement of the classroom, or even the adult–child ratio in the classroom. Accordingly, the issue of professional development experiences that lead to high-quality teaching has received greater prominence, and the idea that more highly trained and expert early educators are key to ensuring positive outcomes for children has come to the forefront (Burchinal, Cryer, Clifford, & Howes, 2002; Early & Winton, 2001; National Institute of Child Health and Human Development Early Child Care Research Network, 1999).

Recently, states have focused their efforts on improving teachers' effectiveness through quality rating systems (QRSs) and associated early childhood educator competencies. Although the latter are propelled by professional development, often QRSs and professional development systems operate independently. The separation between systems can make the process of increasing educator quality complex for policy makers. Moreover, without a clear link between QRSs and professional development systems, the two systems can be difficult for early childhood educators to navigate. Relatively little research has been carried out to examine the efforts that states have undertaken in supporting early childhood educator policies through professional development systems. Focusing on the actions of state agencies with regard to the professional development of their early childhood workforces, this chapter examines the efforts of states to promote integration between QRSs and professional development systems.

The political and financial challenges associated with aligning and implementing the two systems will be explored in three sections. First, the types of state agencies through which professional development policies are implemented are identified, and the bearing that the agency's location has on the types of professional development opportunities offered by states is examined. Next, the ways in which states direct financial resources for professional development are discussed. Finally, the influence of state QRSs on the professional development of the early childhood work force is explored.

THE ROLE OF PROFESSIONAL DEVELOPMENT STANDARDS IN MOVING THE TEACHING WORK-FORCE BEYOND BASIC LICENSING REQUIREMENTS

Current licensing requirements for the professional development of early childhood teachers vary across states, but tend to require little more than a high school degree and a few college-level courses. However, teachers with more formal education provide higher quality experiences for the children they teach (Howes, 1997; National Institute of Child Health and Human Development Early Child Care Research Network, 1996; Phillips, Mekos, Scarr, McCartney, & Abbott-Shim, 2000; Phillipsen, Burchinal, Howes, & Cryer, 1997). Consequently, the type of training and subsequent changes to teacher practices should be carefully considered as part of the professional development system; simply adding more years of education or training does not necessarily predict classroom quality or academic gains for children. Instead, classroom quality and children's academic achievement depend on instructional quality, which may require a variety of professional development supports, including training, mentoring, and formal education, among other activities (Burchinal et al., 2008; Early et al., 2006, 2007, 2008). In addition, increasing teachers' formal training and professional development provides teachers with the opportunity to earn more money and may decrease staff turnover, because earning higher wages and having a greater percentage of highly trained coworkers are related to a decrease in turnover, which is a correlate of child care quality (Whitebook & Sakai, 2003). With these relationships in mind, this section examines how standards established in state QRSs are designed to move teachers past basic licensing requirements for professional development.

Two of the many ways that states structure improvements in professional development are threshold requirements for quality and tiered professional development systems. In the mid-1990s, New Mexico required all teachers to meet a teaching requirement threshold of one 45-hour base-level quality training course. Initially, practitioners in the field resisted the requirement, since it applied to highly trained and experienced teachers as well as newcomers to the field. Not all professionals felt that they required the same level of training. However, after overcoming this initial challenge to establishing a baseline for teacher training and quality improvement, the state began paving the way for future quality improvement initiatives.

Tiered QRSs are an example of a professional structure that by design, moves teachers to higher levels of formal training that exceed basic licensing requirements. Examples of this type of system include the Look for the Stars program in New Mexico and the Delaware Stars program, both of which have licensing requirements as the first and most basic level of the system, dubbed a "one-star" rating. Subsequent levels require teachers to move toward national accreditation standards as the highest levels of staff qualifications and professional development requirements that exceed basic licensing requirements. Another component of tiered QRSs that may provide incentives for teachers to move beyond basic licensing requirements is tiered reimbursement. Tiered reimbursement systems provide higher reimbursement rates for children in classrooms with more highly qualified teachers, which may translate to higher salaries for teachers. For example, in Maryland, a voluntary program affords teachers increased pay for participating in professional development programs. In sum, tiered systems provide an opportunity to raise teacher qualifications without directly changing the basic licensure requirements across the state.

DIRECTION OF TRAINING FUNDS IN QUALITY RATING SYSTEMS: PROMOTING INTEGRATION BETWEEN EARLY CHILDHOOD EDUCATION POLICIES AND PROFESSIONAL DEVELOPMENT

QRSs frequently raise the requirements for teachers' education and professional development; however, the teacher labor market often has inadequate numbers of highly qualified early childhood teachers to immediately meet the QRS standards. High costs of education and training, coupled with low salaries, often discourage early childhood educators from pursuing professional development and advanced training (National Center for Early Development & Learning, 1997; Phillips, Howes, & Whitebook, 1992). To oppose these barriers, Delaware's system is designed to be gradual and progressive so that teachers may pursue professional development and receive credit in a piecemeal fashion to address the barriers to professional development that teachers may face. States may need to consider the lack of available courses for full-time professionals when they need them and the time it will take the professional development infrastructure to establish additional courses, create classroom space, and develop qualified instructors. To increase both participation in professional development and the overall quality of the workforce, many states have increased financial assistance for early care and education providers.

The sources of funding for professional development and the direction of training funds through state departments affect not only the efficacy of implementing early childhood education and integrating it with professional development policies, but also, in turn, the early childhood education work force. Since the goal of professional development efforts is to increase the training and skill levels of early childhood educators, state policy makers are increasingly focusing their policies on raising education and training requirements for these educators. Although this focus is an important first step, policies can have little impact on teacher quality without a clear linkage to the professional development system that supports quality instructional practices.

One way that states have attempted to integrate professional development systems and early childhood education policies is with QRSs. These systems support training and professional development through a variety of funding streams, including providing financial support for teachers, hiring and managing trainers, and creating an online database for professional development activities. QRS training funds have the potential to support the linkage between state early childhood education policies and professional development. By examining how some states chose to organize and direct their funds, this section explores how QRSs may act as the impetus for increased alignment between state early childhood education policies and professional development.

Teachers

Although attending in-service training is important, without a system in place to ensure that professional development is cumulative and substantive, merely attending discrete workshops may not have a direct impact on classroom quality (Guskey, 2000). To ensure that professional development falls into a learning continuum, almost all QRSs use a career ladder. This instrument outlines the education and experience necessary for early childhood educators to increase their qualifications (Ackerman, 2004). Financial support for professional development along a career ladder includes scholarships, vouchers, grants, increases in salary, and other incentives (e.g., additional paid professional development days). The lack of an incentive, financial or otherwise, may be a challenge for teachers who work long hours and have many out-of-work commitments. Thus, tiered reimbursement and other financial support may provide a key motivation for teachers to make the sacrifices necessary to pursue further training and professional development. For example, in Kentucky, Star Achievement Awards are given to educators who complete the professional development associated with each QRS level. As an educator moves up levels, the size of the award increases, from $250 for the first level to $5,000 for the highest level. Star Achievement Awards encourage educators not only to participate in professional development, but to meet QRS goals.

Delaware takes a similar approach, through the use of professional development support grants. These grants can be used only to pay for approved education or professional development associated with the stated Delaware QRS competencies: college courses, required QRS training, and community-based training for center directors, all of which competencies are associated with a tiered early childhood education system. Although the size of the grant differs among star levels, there are increased incentives for educators working in "moving to Star 2" and "moving to Star 5" programs. For example, an educator in a "moving to Star 2" child care program is eligible to receive a much larger grant ($5,450) compared with an educator in a "moving to Star 3" child care program ($2,700). Thus, through the use of a tiered funding scheme, Delaware is able to directly target specific subgroups of educators within programs that offer various levels of quality.

In addition to offering grants, some states operate voucher programs for professional development. For example, Pennsylvania uses a professional development refund voucher program to provide funding. To receive the voucher (with a maximum amount of $3,000), educators must be employed in a program participating in the QRS, and the voucher must be used toward a course in an early childhood degree program. The voucher system supports the linkage between state policies for early childhood education and professional development by limiting participation to only educators working in QRS centers.

Aside from grants and vouchers, there are many other avenues by which states provide financial assistance or incentives for professional development. One of the most common programs is Teacher Education and Compensation Helps (TEACH), which aims to increase the level of education of early childhood teachers by providing scholarships for education as well as bonuses and raises after their coursework is completed. Although it is a national program, TEACH is funded at the state level. Therefore, individual states chose the eligibility criteria for their own TEACH programs.

Of the 22 states that have a TEACH program, only a few have aligned their QRSs with TEACH funds (Child Care Services Association, 2009). In Ohio, educators are eligible for TEACH assistance for an associate's degree only if they are working in a center that either is participating or is not eligible for participation (e.g., a family child care center) in the state's QRS. Even more stringently, educators pursuing a bachelor's degree are eligible for participation in TEACH only if they are working in a state QRS center. Delaware and Kentucky follow a similar model, giving preferential status to educators in QRS programs. By directly linking their systems to the TEACH program, these states promote integration between professional development and early childhood education competencies, at the same time encouraging teachers to seek out employment in programs participating in the QRS. This approach benefits the programs through the increased availability of a more highly qualified work force.

In addition to offering scholarship programs, some states have begun to use wage initiatives to increase educators' participation in professional development. For instance, Maryland awards bonuses to early childhood educators participating in the state's QRS. The state gives a bonus to the educator upon completion of each quality level's professional development requirements. The amount of each bonus increases as educators move up the hierarchy of levels. For example, an educator receives $200 upon completion of first-level requirements and $1,000 upon completion of the highest level. Maryland's bonus system clearly gives educators an incentive to attain the highest level of professional development associated with the QRS.

Trainers

Another method through which a QRS provides professional development opportunities for educators is through supporting and training staff to provide in-service training. States vary in how they fund QRS trainers, offering assistance ranging from scholarships to grants or vouchers. By directly funding and training trainers, state leaders can manage the content and focus of the state's professional development system through the QRS. For example, in Kentucky, trainers are required to hold an Early Care and Education Trainer's credential in order to lead professional development through the QRS. To receive this credential, trainers have to complete a number of seminars and pass a review process. Professional development must be aligned with the state's early childhood competencies before QRS officials approve the professional development session. By directly funding trainers, Kentucky ensures that all professional development is aligned with early childhood education competencies through the QRS.

Pennsylvania also uses QRS funds to promote the quality of professional development. Any trainer who receives funding from the state is required to participate in the Pennsylvania Quality Assurance System, which focuses on the quality of individual trainers as opposed to actual professional development activities. Toward that end, the state funded the creation of three online courses that each trainer is required to take in order to lead any professional development opportunity. For each professional development session, two peer reviewers assess each trainer's professional development plan and give their recommendations to the trainer. Pennsylvania's professional development system supports the alignment between QRS competencies and professional development by managing the content and quality of the latter.

Personnel and Training Registries

To ensure that states are able to track and manage professional development, many states have funded personnel and training registry systems—online databases that systematically link early childhood education competencies to the education and training offered in the state. The registry systems track educators' completed education and professional development and match them against the state's career ladder. Ohio, Pennsylvania, and Delaware have training registries. Pennsylvania's Early Learning Keys to Quality training registry allows educators to register online for professional development opportunities and track their progress on the career ladder. In addition, instructors can post upcoming opportunities and print certificates of attendance. The Ohio Early Childhood Professional Development Network initially collected and tracked the professional development histories of educators employed in programs participating in the state's QRS; in 2006, Ohio expanded the registry to encompass all early childhood educators. QRS funds lay the foundation for a statewide integration between early childhood education competencies and professional development.

In Delaware, the training registry not only tracks the completion of professional development, but also helps stakeholders review educators' qualifications. State policy requires the professional development system to review the qualifications of all professionals employed in early childhood programs. Consequently, allocating funds to organize, track, and manage professional development systems through personnel and training registries supports the linkage between early childhood policies and professional development.

Institutions of Higher Education

Historically, the content in institutions of higher education has been somewhat distinct from state-level early childhood policies. Although states may push for higher education requirements, policies rarely specify course content. In New Mexico, stakeholders in early childhood aligned QRS competencies with institutions of higher education by creating a three-way partnership among higher education, state government, and local trainers. The QRS funded the creation of the Early Childhood Education Task Force, which published a universal catalogue of courses. Course titles and content map directly onto system competencies. All institutions of higher education across the state teach the same courses, with the same title and content, for all undergraduate courses. By funding the universal catalogue of courses, New Mexico is able to ensure that courses taught in institutions of higher education are aligned with QRS competencies.

In sum, the direction of training funds can promote the integration of early childhood education policies and professional development activities by encouraging teachers to take advantage of professional development along a career ladder, requiring trainers to provide training that is aligned with the QRS, and tracking the progress of professional development activities.

AGENCIES IN WHICH PROFESSIONAL DEVELOPMENT SYSTEMS AND QUALITY RATING SYSTEMS ARE HOUSED

The location of the QRS has the potential to drive or thwart the integration between early childhood education policies and professional development activities. Although QRSs typically are housed within a particular state government department, each system often is developed in collaboration with various partners and has a different political oversight that affects its alignment with the professional development system. State departments of education and departments of health and welfare are the most common locations sites for QRSs, but systems vary substantially across states in terms of their linkages with the professional development system.

The first QRS for child care settings was implemented in Oklahoma in 1998 and is housed within the Oklahoma Department of Education. Since then, 19 states have designed and implemented such rating systems to improve the quality of early child care programs. Using a case-study model, this section explores where the QRSs are housed in different states, how such systems were developed, how partnerships and collaborations were created with other agencies, and, finally, how those partnerships influence state policy around both QRSs and professional development systems. The systems described are in place in Pennsylvania, Delaware, Kentucky, Maryland, and New Mexico.

Pennsylvania

Of the states examined in this case study, Pennsylvania was the first to develop and implement a QRS, which started in 2002. Pennsylvania's system, known as Keystone STARS (Standards Training/Professional Development Assistance Resources Support), is housed under the state's Department of Public Welfare. The system was devised in 2002 by Governor Mark Schweiker's office in order to raise quality above minimum licensing requirements, and to improve, support, and recognize the continuous quality improvement efforts of early childhood education programs in Pennsylvania. Governor Schweiker commissioned a task force which charged the Office of Child Development and Early Learning with developing a rating system that would support quality improvement for early childhood programs. Although the system is housed within the Department of Public Welfare rather than the Department of Education, it was created in collaboration with other state departments that were focused on early childhood education. Because of its collaborative focus, Pennsylvania was able to align its QRS with early learning standards and the state's professional development system. For example, Pennsylvania Keystone STARS requires participating early childhood education programs to use a curriculum that is aligned with the state's learning standards for early childhood, which, together with their indicators, are addressed in the state's professional development system, the Pennsylvania Core Body of Knowledge Competencies. These competencies aim to improve child outcomes by improving the quality of early childhood education programs and teaching. In this way, the QRS is linked to the professional development system through the early learning standards and early childhood education competencies.

Delaware

Delaware's QRS, Delaware Stars for Early Success, was implemented in 2005 and is housed in the state Department of Education, through the Office of Early Care and Education. The state's professional development system, Delaware First: Professional Development for Early Childhood, also is housed within the Department of Education. In 2002, the Delaware Interagency Resource Management Committee established the Office of Early Care and Education, with the intent to support the implementation of Early Success, a plan devised to aid the development of a quality early care and education system throughout the state. The Delaware QRS was developed as a public–private partnership comprising the state Department of Education, Department of Health and Social Services, and Department of Services for Children, Youth, and Their Families; The Family & Workplace Connection, a division of Children and Families First; and United Way Success by Six. Delaware is still in the process of fully integrating the highest quality rating and professional development systems. The State faced some challenges in determining the different criteria for advancing through the levels of the QRS and in and building in a professional development component, both conceptually (specifically, in determining the content of the professional development that would map onto the QRS levels) and in the application process of rolling out the linked systems. Currently, the state wants the STARS program to use specific content training modules, and these modules are available throughout Delaware (an online component is being built as well). The state is preparing to move its QRS to the Delaware Institute for Excellence in Early Childhood. After the move takes place, there will be considerable overlap in technical assistance, trainers, and other aspects of the professional development system. In addition, the individuals who are involved with the QRS also work with the professional development system, and the group working on the latter is making an effort to ensure that professional development services are available to programs that participate in the STARS program.

Kentucky

Both Kentucky's QRS, STARS for KIDS (Kentucky Invests in Developing Success) NOW and its professional development system, KIDS NOW, are housed within the state's Department of Education. The systems were established through the collaboration of five professional development work groups, the Professional Development Council, and the Governor's Office of Early Childhood Development. Perhaps because the two systems are housed within the same department, they appear to be well integrated and linked. For example, providers are required to take certain professional development courses before they can increase their level in the tiered QRS. In addition, the Early Learning Standards and course content for professional development are synchronized so that the course content is aligned with what children need to know when entering kindergarten.

Maryland

In Maryland, the Division of Early Childhood Development at the state Department of Education is responsible for early child care and education. The Division houses the Office of Child Care and the Early Learning Branch. In 2001, the Maryland Subcabinet for Children, Youth, and Families, in partnership with the Annie E. Casey Foundation and the Council for Excellence in Government, convened the 40 members of the Leadership in Action Program for the purpose of the accelerating the state's achievement of its school-readiness goals. As in Delaware, Maryland's QRS was developed and implemented in collaboration with privately funded as well as public institutions.

New Mexico

New Mexico's QRS, Look for the Stars, is housed in the Office of Child Development in the Children, Youth and Families Department. New Mexico also has a quality rating improvement system, called AIM HIGH, which targets children from low-income families. The state's licensing and professional development system functions are housed in the Public Education Department. The Office of Early Childhood was housed in the state Department of Education until 1989, when it was moved to the Children, Youth and Families Department. The Office of Child Development is responsible for examining the components of the QRS and for integrating the learning standards and early childhood education competencies. The latter require that early childhood programs establish an environment which provides opportunities and reinforcement for children's practice of healthy behaviors that promote appropriate nutrition and physical and psychological well-being, as well as demonstrate knowledge of the reading and writing components of literacy at each developmental level (a component of curriculum development). Currently, early childhood education competencies are included in higher education coursework so that there is an integration of the QRS and the professional development course content.

Ohio

Ohio's QRS, Step Up to Quality, is located within the Ohio Department of Job and Family Services (ODJFS), Bureau of Child Care and Development, within the state Department of Health. Ohio views these three agencies as interrelated to work together in providing high-quality child care. The QRS began to be developed in 1999 and was fully implemented in 2004. Step Up to Quality is a statewide system that is linked with the state's professional development system. Accordingly, teacher competencies are woven into the system via Career Pathways (a system designed to recognize teachers for their experience, education, credentials and training). The QRS was developed as a public–private partnership comprising the ODJFS, Ohio Child Care Resource and Referral Association, Build Ohio, Ohio Department of Education, and Office of Early Learning and School Readiness. The initial criteria were outlined in 1999–2000, a pilot program was implemented in nine counties in 2005, and statewide implementation occurred in 2006–2007.

The location of a QRS within any government agency can both facilitate and impede the vision and implementation of that system. For example, states that housed these multiple components in one department or had good working relationships between departments had a more streamlined implementation of professional development in relation to the QRS. Therefore, it is important to consider the placement of the two systems with respect to each other, as well as the effect that such placement may have on the implementation and effectiveness of each system.

CONCLUSION

The quality of nonparental care consistently predicts outcomes for young children (Meehan, Hughes, & Cavell, 2003; Pianta et al., 2005). Recently, state governments have actively pursued policies and programs that focus on the training and professional development of educators and the requirements and procedures for identifying who is qualified to teach. With the influx of policies related to professional development, there has been little reflection on the impact of state agencies' choices. This chapter has presented several case studies of how state agencies have chosen to support professional development through the state's QRS.

Although many states have ambitious goals for moving teachers beyond basic licensing requirements, this goal can be difficult to obtain without a clear system in place to support the growth and quality of professional development. Some states have thoughtfully allocated funding streams to give educators an incentive to participate in professional development and to manage its quality and content. Through a systematic management of funding, state agencies have promoted the alignment of early childhood education competencies and professional development activities.

Efforts to link professional development and early childhood education policies through a QRS vary by state. Often, where state agencies chose to house the QRS influences the integration between professional development and early childhood education competencies. State actions in pursuit of creating a collaborative infrastructure between typically separate organizations tend to promote integration. By streamlining activities, educators can easily navigate the professional development system and exceed states' basic licensing requirements. Examining state agencies' choices related to QRSs demonstrates the potential for states to promote the integration of these systems with professional development systems. However, state agencies vary greatly in their efforts to improve the early childhood work force. Because QRSs are relatively new, several key challenges lie ahead for stakeholders in such systems to improve the quality of early childhood educators:

1. Policy makers should consider giving teachers incentives to move beyond basic licensing requirements for professional development. This may be accomplished through increased pay incentives, scholarships, and other reward programs. Furthermore, policy makers should ensure that early childhood educators have access to professional development opportunities during nontraditional work hours or should consider sponsoring release time for teachers to pursue professional development training.

2. In addition to concentrating on the completion of professional development and aligning it with core competencies, policy makers need to focus on its content and quality. Although some states have begun to pay attention to the quality of trainers, further effort is needed to manage actual professional development activities. Kentucky's review process is a good example of how a state can control the quality of each professional development experience.

3. States need to create clear partnerships among organizations. Without this, policy makers face an uphill battle in integrating early childhood education policies and professional development. By collaborating across agencies, states can ensure that the two are aligned under one cohesive vision.

Stakeholders across the country have implemented successful policies and programs to improve the quality of early childhood educators. As QRSs continue to grow and develop, educators and policy makers will increase their potential to greatly influence the early childhood work force. To achieve the most advantageous results, they should carefully consider how to best design and align professional development systems and QRSs through a well-thought-out and well-developed plan.

STUDY QUESTIONS

1. What is a threshold requirement within a QRS? Give an example relevant to professional development.

2. What are tiered professional development systems?

3. What is in-service training? Give two examples of in-service training systems.

REFERENCES

Ackerman, D.J. (2004). States' efforts in improving the qualifications of early care and education teachers. *Educational Policy, 18*(2), 311–337.

Burchinal, M.R., Cryer, D., Clifford, R.M., & Howes, C. (2002). Caregiver training and classroom quality in child care centers. *Applied Developmental Science, 6,* 2–11.

Burchinal, M.R., Howes, C., Pianta, R., Bryant, D., Early, D., Clifford, R., et al. (2008). Predicting child outcomes at the end of kindergarten from the quality of pre-kindergarten teacher–child interactions and instruction. *Applied Developmental Science, 12*(3), 140–153.

Child Care Services Association. (2009). Creating systems of support for the early childhood workforce: T.E.A.C.H. Early Childhood and Child Care WAGE$ national annual program report (pp. 1–7). Chapel Hill, NC: Author.

Early, D., & Winton, P. (2001). Preparing the workforce: Early childhood teacher preparation at 2- and 4-year institutes of higher education. *Early Childhood Research Quarterly, 16,* 285–306.

Early, D.M., Bryant, D., Pianta, R., Clifford, R.M., Burchinal, M.R., Ritchie, S., et al. (2006). Are teacher's education, major, and credentials related to classroom quality and children's academic gains in pre-kindergarten? *Early Childhood Research Quarterly, 21,* 174–195.

Early, D.M., Maxwell, K.L., Burchinal, M., Alva, S., Bender, R.H., Bryant, D., et al. (2007). Teachers' education, classroom quality, and young children's academic skills: Results from seven studies of preschool programs. *Child Development, 78*(2), 558–580.

Early, D.M., Maxwell, K.L., Clifford, R.M., Pianta, R.C., Ritchie, S., Howes, C., et al. (2008). Policy commentary. *Early Childhood Research Quarterly, 23,* 7–9.

Guskey, T. (2000). *Evaluating professional development.* Thousand Oaks, CA: Corwin Press.

Howes, C. (1997). Children's experiences in center-based child care as a function of teacher background and adult:child ratios. *Merrill-Palmer Quarterly, 43,* 404–425.

Howes, C., Burchinal, M., Pianta, R., Bryant, D., Early, D., Clifford, R., et al. (2008). Ready to learn? Children's preacademic achievement in pre-kindergarten programs. *Early Childhood Research Quarterly, 23*(1), 27–50.

Mashburn, A.J., Pianta, R.C., Hamre, B.K., Downer, J.T., Barbarin, O.A., Bryant, D., et al. (2008). Measures of classroom quality in prekindergarten and children's development of academic, language, and social skills. *Child Development, 79*(3), 732–749.

Meehan, B.T., Hughes, J.N., & Cavell, T.A. (2003). Teacher–student relationships as compensatory resources for aggressive children. *Child Development, 74,* 1145–1157.

National Center for Early Development & Learning. (1997). How are legislative policies affecting our children? *Early Developments, 1*(3), 1–16.

National Institute of Child Health and Human Development, Early Child Care Research Network. (1996). Characteristics of infant child care: Factors contributing to positive caregiving. *Early Childhood Research Quarterly, 11,* 269–306.

National Institute of Child Health and Human Development, Early Child Care Research Network. (1999). Child outcomes when child care centers meet recommended standards for quality. *American Journal for Public Health, 89*(7), 1072–1077.

Phillips, D.A., Howes, C., & Whitebook, M. (1992). The social policy context of child care: Effects on quality. *American Journal of Community Psychology, 20*(1), 25–51.

Phillips, D.A., Mekos, D., Scarr, S., McCartney, K., & Abbott-Shim, M. (2000).Within and beyond the classroom door: Assessing quality in childcare centers. *Early Childhood Research Quarterly, 15,* 475–496.

Phillipsen, L.C., Burchinal, M.R., Howes, C., & Cryer, D. (1997). The prediction of process quality from structural features of child care. *Early Childhood Research Quarterly, 12,* 281–303.

Pianta, R., Howes, C., Burchinal, M., Bryant, D., Clifford, R., Early, D., et al. (2005). Features of pre-kindergarten programs, classrooms, and teachers: Do they predict observed classroom quality and child–teacher interactions? *Applied Developmental Science, 9*(3), 144–159.

Whitebook, M., & Sakai, L. (2003). Turnover begets turnover: An examination of job and occupational instability among child care center staff. *Early Childhood Research Quarterly, 18,* 273–293.

7

Evaluating the Integration of Systems on Effective Teaching, Classroom Environments, and Children's Preacademic Learning

Promjawan Udommana, Jill Haak, and Tamar Mintz

A quality rating system (QRS), sometimes called a quality rating and improvement system(QRIS), is a mechanism for defining the optimal conditions for caring for children, preparing them for school, and encouraging and rewarding their improvement to higher levels. Such a system utilizes a building-block approach in which every quality level consists of a particular benchmark. Six states—Delaware, Kentucky, Maryland, New Mexico, Ohio, and Pennsylvania—use QRSs in five main areas: staff-to-child ratios and class size, professional development, classroom environment, parental involvement, and management and administration.

A professional development system, by contrast, is a set of requirements and procedures by which states determine who is qualified to teach, together with the mechanisms for preparing, training, and qualifying teachers. In most states, teacher qualification is based on credential, degree, and training experience, but it also depends on the type of program (e.g., center based, family child care center) and the position of the candidate (e.g., director, practitioner, lead teacher). Similar to the building-block approach in a QRS, professional development systems in some states (Pennsylvania, New Mexico, Ohio) offer a career lattice that defines appropriate levels of education and credentials for various positions in the early care and education field. Early childhood professionals can move up to a higher rung on the career lattice when they meet the requirements set at that level. Theoretically, the professional development system is embedded in the QRS, since one of the areas of the latter involves teacher qualification.

In this chapter, we address the issue of evaluating QRSs and professional development systems. First, we define structural elements of each system that are common to the six states examined. Then we propose an evaluation plan that is based on examining differential teaching and child outcomes across structural levels. Finally, using existing evaluation research in Kentucky and Pennsylvania, state-funded preschool impact studies in New Mexico and Maryland, and the structure of other state systems, we explore the specific challenges of evaluation and the next steps for evaluation studies.

THE OVERARCHING THEMES OF AN EVALUATION PLAN

Establishing a QRS and a professional development system is the first step in improving early childhood education (Howes et al., 2008). An important next step is to implement program evaluation research in order to understand whether programs at different star levels or teachers with more advanced credentials affect child outcomes and whether these credentials actually translate to more effective teaching practices and positive classroom environments. New Mexico, Kentucky, Pennsylvania, and Maryland have begun to evaluate the effectiveness of various aspects of their programs. Their evaluation plans differ on the basis of whether state or independent researchers are conducting the research, what parts of the program are being reviewed, and what outcomes are being measured, but the simple fact that the programs *are* being evaluated is key. Both state and independent researchers have begun the research. The National Institute for Early Education Research at Rutgers University conducted the first evaluation research in New Mexico, the University of Pittsburgh and the University of Pennsylvania carried out the evaluation research in Pennsylvania, and the University of Kentucky conducted it in Kentucky (Barnard, Smith, Fiene, & Swanson, 2006; Hustedt, Barnett, Jung, & Figueras, 2008; Kentucky Department of Education, 2004, 2007, 2008). In contrast, the Maryland State Department of Education conducted the evaluation research in Maryland, and the Delaware State Department of Education initiated research in its state (Noble, 2009; Maryland State Department of Education, 2004). University, state, and private entities provide multiple options for states to pursue funding and support in conducting evaluation research.

Most state evaluation studies look only at prekindergarten in general or at a particular type of prekindergarten program; only Pennsylvania has investigated whether stars or levels predict outcomes. It is important to understand this association, because it drives many quality rating and professional development systems. The selection of outcome measures also illustrates the complexity of defining a program's effectiveness. In selecting outcomes, states must determine whether they want to measure teaching practices, classroom environments, child outcomes, or some combination of these factors. In addition, they must think about measures that will most appropriately represent the effects of each of these variables. Finally, it is important for future evaluation research to consider the many moderating factors that may be influencing outcomes and to collect data on them. Many factors contribute to how a child performs on a given day. Demographic factors such as gender, socioeconomic status, ethnicity, and maternal education are known to have an effect on outcome scores (Hamre & Pianta, 2005; LoCasale-Crouch et al., 2007; National Institute of Child Health and Human Development, 2002). Individual and family physical, psychological, and behavioral factors also influence performance (Bos, Coleman, & Vaughn, 2002; Hinshaw, 1992; Shonkoff & Phillips, 2000). It is important to consider these multiple factors, in addition to child care and education factors, in child outcome evaluation studies. Understanding whether a child's characteristics or other external factors are influencing outcomes will be important in terms of looking forward and designing programs to buffer against risk factors.

Various study designs may be employed, and evaluation research should carefully decide on the most appropriate protocol. For example, using a regression discontinuity design to control for selection bias, the National Institute for Early Education Research at Rutgers University is reviewing child outcome data comparing children who have completed the prekindergarten program with children who are just beginning the program (Hustedt et al., 2008). By contrast, both Maryland and Pennsylvania used a standard multiple-group comparison design to study prekindergarten children (Maryland State Department of Education, 2004). The research methods should be driven by a consideration of what the research aims to measure, such as the effects of rating levels on child outcomes or the impact of teacher credentials on child outcomes.

METHODOLOGY AND RESEARCH DESIGN OF THE EVALUATION STUDIES

Among the six states that were examined, five evaluation studies were conducted in four states: Kentucky, Pennsylvania, New Mexico, and Maryland. (See Table 7.1.) Evaluation studies of the states' QRS are available in Kentucky and Pennsylvania, and studies of the quality of child care

Table 7.1. Summary table of the evaluation studies

State	Evaluator/year	Research design	Sample	Measures: Classroom quality	Measures: Child outcome	Other indicators
Kentucky	University of Kentucky, 2004	Descriptive study	Center-based child care programs 1) Infant/toddler classroom 2) Preschool classroom	ELLCO ITERS-R ECERS-R	None	Child's family background Director and staff education Urban and rural differences
	University of Kentucky, 2007		Types of programs 1) Head Start 2) Nonprofit 3) For profit	ECERS-R ELLCO ITERS-R	PPVT-III WJ-III	Child's family background Child's age group
Pennsylvania	University of Pittsburgh, Pennsylvania State University, 2006	Descriptive study	Types of programs 1) 356 child care centers 2) 81 group child care homes 3) 135 family child care homes	ECERS-R FDCRS	None	Curriculum Teacher quality 1) Degree and credential 2) Teaching experience 3) Professional development requirement
New Mexico	Rutgers University, 2008	Two group comparison using regression-discontinuity design	Types of programs 1) 519 children in prekindergarten classrooms 2) 405 children in kindergarten classrooms		PPVT-III TVIP WJ-III Batería Woodcock–Muñoz Pruebas de Approvechamiento–Revisado TOPEL Pre-CTOPP	Child's ethnicity Family incomes
Maryland	Maryland State Department of Education, 2004	Multiple group comparison	Types of prior care experience (selected from the predominant form of care) 1) 5,527 children with child care center 2) 1,695 children with family child care 3) 4,005 children with Head Start 4) 6,779 children with nonpublic nursery 5) 16,796 children with prekindergarten 6) 1,242 children with kindergarten repeat		School readiness skills: social & personal, language & literacy, math thinking, social studies, arts, and physical development	Combination of two types of care Disabilites

Key: ECERS-R, Early Childhood Environment Rating Scale, Revised; ELLCO, Early Language and Literacy Classroom Observation Tool; FDCRS, Family Day Care Rating Scale; ITERS-R, Infant–Toddler Environment Scale, Revised; PPVT-III, Peabody Picture Vocabulary Test; PPVT-III, Peabody Picture Vocabulary Test, Third Edition; Pre-CTOPP, Preschool Comprehensive Test of Phonological and Print Processing; TOPEL, Test of Preschool Literacy; TVIP, Test de Vocabulario en Imagenes Peabody; WJ-III, Woodcock-Johnson Tests of Achievement, Third Edition.

programs are available in New Mexico and Maryland. Delaware and Ohio are in the process of conducting such studies.

The Overall Methodology and Research Design

The research design of the six states' evaluation studies fall into two categories: a descriptive study examining factors associated with classroom quality and a comparative study of two or multiple groups of children that examines their outcomes from previous child care experience. The evaluation studies conducted in Kentucky and Pennsylvania were descriptive studies, whereas the ones conducted in New Mexico and Maryland used a comparative approach.

Among the instruments used to examine classroom quality were the Early Childhood Environment Rating Scale, Revised (ECERS-R; Harms, Clifford, & Cryer, 1998), the Infant–Toddler Environment Scale, Revised (ITERS-R; Harms, Cryer, & Clifford, 2006), and the Early Language and Literacy Classroom Observation Tool (ELLCO; Smith & Dickinson, 2002). Both the ECERS-R and the ITERS-R are used to assess classroom quality in center-based child care. The ECERS-R is commonly used to assess quality in a preschool classroom, and the ITERS-R is used to access quality in an infant–toddler classroom. The two instruments have seven subscales: Space and Furnishing, Personal Care and Routine, Language Reasoning (in the ECERS-R) or Listening and Talking (in the ITERS-R), Activities, Interactions, Program Structure, and Parent and Staff. The instrument used to examine quality in a family child care home was the Family Day Care Rating Scale (FDCRS; Harms, Clifford, & Cryer, 1989). The FDCRS uses the same format as the ECERS-R and includes the following seven subscales: Space and Furnishing of Care and Learning, Basic Care, Language and Reasoning, Learning Activities, Social Development, Adult Needs, and Provision for Exceptional Children. The ELLCO measures teacher–child interactions specific to language and literacy learning.

The child outcome assessments in the evaluation studies across the four states focus on school readiness skills such as receptive vocabulary, mathematics, and early literacy skills. Among these measures are the Peabody Picture Vocabulary Test, Third Edition (PPVT-III; Dunn & Dunn, 1997); Test de Vocabulario en Imágenes Peabody (TVIP; Dunn, Padilla, Lugo, & Dunn, 1986); Woodcock-Johnson Tests of Achievement, Third Edition (WJ-III; Woodcock, McGrew, & Mather, 2001); Batería Woodcock–Muñoz Pruebas de Approvechamiento–Revisado (Woodcock & Muñoz, 1990); Test of Preschool Literary (TOPEL; Lonigan, Wagner, Torgesen, & Rashotte, 2007); and Preschool Comprehensive Test of Phonological and Print Processing (Pre-CTOPP; Lonigan, Wagner, &

Rashotte, 2002). Maryland uses a school readiness score that is relevant to the Maryland Model for School Readiness.

Despite the similarity of their choice of child assessment measures, each state uses other, unique indicators to examine the quality of its child care program. For example, Maryland considers the combination of different types of care matter for school readiness skills. Kentucky and New Mexico include a child individual-level variable such as family income, ethnicity, and age difference to examine the classroom interactions of a particular group of children. Kentucky and New Mexico also consider teacher characteristics and curriculum in conducting their QRS evaluation studies.

BACKGROUND AND RESULTS OF SOME EVALUATION STUDIES

The discussion that follows offers some interesting examples that provide useful detailed information about the backgrounds and results of evaluation studies carried out in the states examined for this study.

Kentucky

Kentucky's QRS is called STARS for KIDS (Kentucky Invests in Developing Success) NOW. A four-tiered voluntary system for improving center-based child care and family child care homes, STARS for KIDS NOW is administered by the Cabinet for Health and Family Services in the Division of Child Care. Each of the four levels requires programs to go above and beyond the minimum state licensing requirements. One star indicates that an early childhood program has made a commitment to quality by entering the STARS for KIDS NOW program. Four stars indicate that the participating early childhood program has achieved the highest quality. Programs are assessed on their staff-to-child ratios and class size, curriculum, education and training of staff, and personnel practices (Kentucky Department of Education, 2008a).

In order to support early childhood professional growth and development, the framework guiding the professional development system in Kentucky involves five levels of professional accomplishment and training, technical assistance, credentialing, and articulations agreements that support each level (Rous, Howard, Chance, DeJohn, & Hoover, 2008). Both the professional development system and the QRS are parts of the STARS for KIDS NOW initiative that aims to establish supports and services to ensure children's well-being in Kentucky (Rous, McCormick, Gooden, & Townley, 2007).

The Universities of Kentucky and Louisville collaborated to conduct an evaluation of STARS for KIDS NOW in 2004. Multiple data sources, including surveys, face-to-face interviews, and classroom observations, were used. A number of findings emerged from this evaluation. First, the overall quality of classrooms in center-based child care in the state was lower than in the previous year. Second, infant and toddler classrooms achieved higher scores than preschool classrooms on the ITERS-R and ECERS-R. Third, programs accredited by either the National Association for the Education of Young Children or Head Start had the highest quality rating scores according to the ITERS-R, ECERS-R, and ELLCO. Fourth, the quality of care was lower in centers that served a larger percentage of minority children and children who were receiving child care subsidies.

In terms of the impact of the STARS for KIDS NOW on early childhood programs, programs whose staff were more familiar with STARS for KIDS NOW and whose teachers were more highly educated tended to have higher quality classrooms. In particular, the levels of education of the director and staff were positively correlated with literacy and language environments in prekindergarten classrooms. Moreover, rural programs were more familiar with the components of the program and were more likely to participate in it than were urban programs. Rural centers also had higher literacy instruction scores than urban programs (Kentucky Department of Education, 2004).

A second evaluation of STARS for KIDS NOW was conducted in 2006–2007. As was found in 2004, program type made a difference in overall classroom quality. Among preschool classrooms, Head Start programs scored significantly higher in classroom quality on the ECERS-R and the ELLCO than did other types of programs. Moreover, for infant–toddler classrooms, nonprofit programs scored higher than for-profit programs. Children in nonprofit centers scored significantly higher than children in for-profit programs on all child outcome measures, including a letter-naming task, counting, and letter–word identification.

The evidence shows that there is an overall trend toward increased preschool classroom quality over time. Furthermore, there are similarities between high-performing centers. For example, centers performing in the 25th percentile in overall classroom quality reported similar levels of participation in STARS for KIDS NOW. Thus, the findings of the evaluation study indicate that participation in the STARS for KIDS NOW initiative improves classroom quality for preschool programs (Kentucky Department of Education, 2007).

Pennsylvania

Pennsylvania's Keystone Standards, Training/Professional Development, Assistance, Resources, and Support (STARS) is a four-tiered QRS. Programs are evaluated on the basis of their staff qualifications and professional development, children's outcomes after participating in a program, the program environment, programs' partnerships with families and communities, and their leadership and management (Pennsylvania Departments of Public Welfare and Education, 2009). Keystone STARS is managed through a partnership between the Office of Child Development and Early Learning and the Pennsylvania and Regional Keys (Pennsylvania Key, n.d.).

Pennsylvania has a professional development system called the Pennsylvania Keys to Professional Development. This system defines a core body of knowledge about early childhood, qualifications and credentials, quality assurances, access, outreach, and funding. Pennsylvania also provides an Early Learning Career Lattice, which guides the education of staff and the director. When staff or the director makes progress up the career lattice (comprising Levels 1–8), their achievement helps the program earn and maintain a star rating (Pennsylvania Departments of Public Welfare and Education, 2009).

The evaluation study of the Keystone STARS was conducted in 2006. The purposes of the study were to examine the improvement in child care programs after they had participated in the Keystone STARS (Barnard et al., 2006). The data used in this evaluation study were gathered by the Pennsylvania Department of Public Welfare's Office of Child Development. Analysis was performed by the University of Pittsburgh and the Pennsylvania State University. The sites that participated in the study were 356 child care centers, 81 group child care homes, and 135 family child care homes. These 572 sites were randomly selected from child care centers and family child care homes that were not participating in any STARS program or accreditation and from centers that requested the Environment Rating Scale Validating Visit, as part of the STARS designation process or as part of their participation in Keystone STARS. Center-based programs were assessed with the ECERS-R, and home-based programs were assessed with the FDCRS.

The study found that both center- and home-based child care practitioners with higher STARS ratings had consistently higher scores on the ECERS-R scale. In particular, centers which reported that they used a standardized curriculum scored significantly higher on the ECERS-R. This trend also was observed in the family child care homes. Furthermore, teachers and family child care practitioners who had more experience working in early childhood settings and who had received higher education provided higher quality early care and education than did teachers and practitioners who had less experience and lower levels of education. Consequently, the quality of child care programs increased after they participated in Keystone STARS.

New Mexico

New Mexico's QRS, Look for the Stars, is a five-level voluntary rating system. The first level is required for licensing. Subsequent levels are voluntary and enable programs to receive subsidies. Programs are evaluated on the basis of whether they satisfy six criteria: staff training and education, classroom environment, teacher–child ratio and class size, family involvement plan, assessment of children's progress, and learning activities. Look for the Stars includes the criteria of the Aim High Essential Elements in the system's child care licensing requirements. Aim High Essential Elements is a part of the Aim High initiative, developed by the Children, Youth, and Families Department, Office of Child Development, in 1999 (Children, Youth, and Families Department of New Mexico, 2008).

New Mexico Professional Development is the state's professional development system. The Children, Youth, and Families Department of the Office of Child Development collaborated with the State Department of Education, Department of Health, and Department of Labor and with the higher education and community program to establish the New Mexico Five-Year Early Childhood Professional Development Plan in 2007. As of this writing, the state is the final phase of developing the plan (New Mexico Early Childhood Education Professional Development, 2010b). New Mexico Professional Development offers a career lattice consisting of six levels, ranging from a 45-hour entry level course to a master's degree in early childhood care and education (New Mexico Early Childhood Education Professional Development, 2010a).

A 2008 study indicated that children who participated in New Mexico's prekindergarten initiative received better scores in vocabulary, math, and early literacy than did children who had not participated in the initiative. By the beginning of kindergarten, children's vocabulary scores, as measured by the PPVT-III (Dunn & Dunn, 1997), had increased by about 6 raw points after their participation in the program. This increase represents an improvement of about 25% of the standard deviation of the control group, a finding that is particularly important because the measure of vocabulary that was used is predictive of both general cognitive abilities and later success in reading.

The children's early math scores also increased by more than 2 raw points after their participation in the prekindergarten initiative, as measured by the WJ-III (Woodcock et al., 2001). This finding corresponds to an improvement of about 50% of the standard deviation of the control group. The early math skills that were assessed included simple addition and subtraction, basic number concepts, telling time, and counting money.

On the Print Knowledge subtest of the TOPEL (Lonigan et al., 2007), children who participated in the prekindergarten program earned scores that were 14 percentage points higher than children who did not participate. This difference represents an improvement of about 59% of the standard deviation of the control group. Children who attended the program knew more letters, recognized more letter–sound associations, and were more familiar with words and book concepts upon entry to kindergarten than did children who did not attend the program. Across the three domains that were assessed, the differences observed were both statistically significant and practically meaningful (Hustedt et al., 2008).

Maryland

Maryland Child Care Tiered Reimbursement is a four-tiered voluntary system for improving center-based child care and family child care homes. The system evaluates five domains: staff credentialing and training, learning environment, parent involvement, program evaluation, and staff compensation. Child care providers receive incentives for achieving new levels. Child care facilities also receive reimbursement for child care vouchers through the Purchase of Child Care program, a child care subsidy that assists low-income families (Maryland Child Care Resource Network, 2005). Another early childhood program improvement initiative in Maryland is the Maryland State Department of Education (MSDE) Standards for Implementing Quality Early Childhood Programs (Maryland State Department of Education, 2007). Aiming to accredit and define standards across different types of programs including child care, Head Start, and public school early childhood programs, the MSDE programs focus on administration, operation, and family/community partnership. The early childhood programs are rated as accredited or validated; having received conditional, pending accreditation (if the program meets many, but not all, of the standards); or not accredited. The Maryland Child Care Credential System, the professional development system in the state, offers six levels for earning credentials that recognize child care staff members' and administrators' content-specific training hours, coursework, degrees, years of experience, and professional activities (Maryland State Department of Education, 2009b).

In 2004, the state Department of Education conducted a study to examine the association between previous early care experiences and school readiness skills. The data used in this study were collected from 52,130 children who had already enrolled in the kindergarten programs and on whom school readiness information was available. Previous early care experiences included child care centers, family child care, Head Start, nonpublic nurseries, prekindergarten, and home or informal care. The composite school readiness score was based on seven domains of learning:

social and personal skills, language and literacy, mathematical thinking, scientific thinking, social studies, the arts, and physical development.

The Maryland study produced three major results that are relevant to this chapter. First, the study found that approximately three quarters (74%) of children from nonpublic nursery programs demonstrated school readiness, whereas less than half of Head Start children (45%) did. Moreover, children who had been previously enrolled in child care centers or prekindergarten programs performed as well as did the overall kindergarten population. Second, low-income children who had been enrolled in any type of early childhood education program had better school readiness scores than did children who lacked any previous early childhood education experience. In particular, low-income children from nursery schools performed best, followed by low-income children from prekindergarten programs, child care centers, Head Start, and family child care programs, respectively. Finally, among children who received two types of previous care, prekindergarten and Head Start children who were also enrolled at child care centers showed improved school readiness skills, probably because of their additional experience in a regulated early care program (Maryland State Department of Education, 2004).

OVERALL RESULTS FROM THE EVALUATION STUDIES

Within the framework of QRSs and professional development systems, both program quality and teacher quality can be defined by the achievement of each benchmark at each level and can be improved through a systematic upgrade. The common areas used to assess quality at each level in the QRSs are staff-to-child ratios and class size, professional development, classroom environment, parental involvement, and management and administration. Moreover, the quality of each level in a QRS is related to children's experience in a classroom and to social and academic outcomes.

The promising concept of quality improvement has proven to be effective by two evaluation studies, one conducted in Pennsylvania and the other in Kentucky. Both states confirmed that their QRSs were valid and help early childhood programs improve their overall classroom quality and child school readiness skills (Barnard et al., 2006; Kentucky Department of Education, 2008a). Their success may result from the fact that both states include an environment rating scale such as ECERS, ITERS, or FDCRS as a program assessment component in the QRS (Kentucky Department of Education; Pennsylvania Departments of Public Welfare and Education, 2009). Moreover, Pennsylvania also includes assessment tools such as the Ounce Scale and the Work Sampling System in the QRS. These assessment tools are important because they allow researchers to capture children's direct experiences in a classroom, monitor children's progress, and provide information to teachers that will help them plan curricula and inform their training.

Although evaluation studies of other states' QRSs are not yet available, the studies of state-funded preschool impacts in New Mexico and Maryland show similar associations between high quality and children's academic gains, on the one hand (Hustedt et al., 2008), and better school readiness skills, on the other (Maryland State Department of Education, 2004). In the study by Hustedt and colleagues, children who had participated in the New Mexico initiative showed greater academic gains than children who did not participate. Moreover, a study conducted in Maryland shows that children who are enrolled in regulated center-based care develop better school readiness than children in home or informal care—especially children from low-income families (Maryland State Department of Education). The 2009–2010 Maryland School Readiness Report shows that the number of children who were defined as fully ready to learn in a kindergarten program in Maryland has consistently increased from the years 2002–2003 to 2009–2010 as a result of the program improvement initiatives (Maryland State Department of Education, 2009a). In sum, all these studies show the beneficial associations between QRSs, professional development systems, and classroom quality, on the one hand, and children's social and academic outcomes, on the other.

CHALLENGES AND NEXT STEPS

Beginning in 1998, 19 states implemented statewide QRSs (Child Care Bureau, 2009). With their ultimate goal of improving quality and ensuring ongoing improvement of early childhood programs and professionals, QRSs are highly political and involve a prodigious financial investment and public awareness, as well as collaborations among different stakeholders. From a research standpoint, an evaluation study is a tool for assessing the impact of QRSs. Thus, researchers need to consider appropriate measures, the sensitivity to the population being served, and the research design when they examine the association between complex and interrelated components in early childhood education programs and child experiences in a classroom, on the one hand, and social and academic outcomes, on the other.

Challenges for Teacher Quality

The quality of early childhood professionals who participate in QRSs and professional development systems is often measured by their credentials, degrees, types of training, and attendance at professional development workshops. Within this framework, the more knowledge teachers gain about early childhood development and education, by receiving a higher degree or attending more professional development workshops, the better the quality of the classroom will be.

Teacher quality, in fact, encompasses a broad range of knowledge, skills, and behaviors (Early et al., 2007) and is influenced by the teachers' beliefs about what and how children learn (adult-centered versus child-centered approach, academic-focused versus relationship-focused learning) (Pianta et al., 2005; Wishard, Shivers, Howes, & Ritchie, 2003). However, more effective teachers also report less stress and depression (Raver et al., 2008). Therefore, it may be challenging to measure teacher quality and the ways in which teachers translate their learning or training into classroom practice in the hopes of learning how teacher quality is related to credentials, degrees, and training, because teacher quality is affected by other, perhaps unknown or unmeasurable, underlying factors..

The professional development systems of the states examined in this chapter demonstrate an increased awareness of the complexity of teacher quality. Most of those states have developed a technical assistance system to support early childhood professionals. Through continuous monitoring, consultation, mentoring, and collaboration between assistant providers and teachers, teachers sustain skills and practices in the field. Some states have taken a further step, providing a personalized technical assistance system to fit teachers' individual needs and requests (Rous et al., 2008). Whichever approach is adopted, a technical assistance system is an ideal way of connect training to practices and regularly assessing teacher performance. The next step is a large-scale evaluation study to map an ongoing teacher support system onto a QRS and then examine the association between the teacher support system and children's experience in the classroom.

Challenges for Program Features

In most states, the programs volunteer to be rated, and the rating is used to rate overall quality in the different types of center-based programs (e.g., prekindergarten, child care center, Head Start program). One of the assumptions of a QRS is that classrooms may operate similarly across different types of programs. In other words, similar standards would benefit children equally, regardless of the programs in which they were enrolled. However, quality is a multilevel and multidimensional construct that includes various program and classroom features (Mashburn et al., 2008).

Features of early childhood programs can differ by location and type of program. For example, prekindergarten classrooms located in a school and taught by teachers earning higher wages spent more time on whole-group instruction than did prekindergarten classrooms outside the school compound (Pianta et al., 2005). Moreover, because eligibility for some early childhood programs (e.g., Head Start) is based on family income, the program determines which group of children will be served. Poverty, teacher–child ethnic differences, the child's English-language proficiency, and the program's focus affect classroom quality (Hamre & Pianta, 2005; LoCasale-Crouch et al., 2007; Wishard et al., 2003).

Existing evaluation studies commonly consider the categorization of family-based child care versus center-based child care to be part and parcel of the variability of programs. However, an increased sensitivity to different program features is needed in future evaluations. The location of the program, the type of program (e.g., Head Start, private preschool, prekindergarten), and the population that is served need to be considered in order to examine how QRSs and professional development systems operate in different classrooms and promote achievement by children from diverse backgrounds.

SUMMARY AND CONCLUSION

Evaluating the effectiveness of QRSs and professional development systems on child outcomes is a critical, but complex, component of improving early childhood education. Multiple states have put early education theory into practice by developing these two kinds of systems and encouraging early childhood providers to participate in, and take advantage of, the opportunities they offer. The systems are based on a theory of what is important for improvement in early child care, but their translation into improved classroom quality, teaching practice, and child outcomes has only begun to be measured. Preliminary research in Kentucky, Pennsylvania, New Mexico, and Maryland highlights the complexity of assessing the effectiveness of such programs, especially with regard to the importance of considering demographic and individual child, family, and teacher characteristics that affect outcomes. Understanding the impact of these variables through evaluation research is crucial in improving QRSs and professional development systems to the point where they address those factors. Evaluation studies in Kentucky and Pennsylvania support the hypothesis that QRSs improve classroom quality. Implementing statewide QRSs and professional development systems is expensive and time and labor intensive. Examining the impact of these programs is essential to understanding whether they are in fact influencing change and in determining how to improve the programs to reach desired outcomes.

STUDY QUESTIONS

1. Name and define four dimensions of difference in evaluation plans.

2. Why is it important to include child outcomes in an evaluation?

3. Based on the material in this chapter, how effective are states in using QRSs to ensure effective teachers?

REFERENCES

Barnard, W., Smith, W.E., Fiene, R., & Swanson, K. (2006). *Evaluation of Pennsylvania's Keystone STARS quality rating system in child care settings.* Harrisburg: Pennsylvania Office of Child Development.

Bos, C.A., Coleman, M., & Vaughn, S. (2002). Reading and students with E/BD: What do we know and recommend? In K.L. Lane, F.M. Gresham, & T.E. O'Shaughnessy (Eds.), *Interventions for children with or at risk for emotional and behavioral disorders* (pp. 87–103). Boston: Allyn & Bacon.

Child Care Bureau. (2009, March). *Quality rating system: Definition and statewide system.* Retrieved May 5, 2009, from http://nccic.acf.hhs.gov/pubs/qrs-defsystems.html

Children, Youth, and Families Department of New Mexico. (2008, July). *Aim High: Essential elements of quality.* Retrieved May 15, 2009, from https://www.newmexicokids.org/Resource/Library/AIMHIGH/AH_EEs_JULY_2008.pdf

Dunn, L.M., & Dunn, L.M. (1997). *Peabody Picture Vocabulary Test-Third Edition (PPVT-III).* Circle Pines, MN: American Guidance Service.

Dunn, L.M., Padilla E.R., Lugo, D.E., & Dunn, L.M. (1986). *Test de Vocabulario en Imágenes Peabody.* Circle Pines, MN: American Guidance Service.

Early, D., Maxwell, K., Burchinal, M., Bender, R., Ebanks, C., Henry, G., et al. (2007). Teacher's education, classroom quality, and young children's academic skills: Results from seven studies of preschool programs. *Child Development, 78*(2), 558–580.

Hamre, B.K., & Pianta, R.C. (2005). Can instructional and emotional support in the first grade classroom make a difference for children at risk of school failure? *Child Development, 76*(5), 949–967.

Harms, T., Clifford, R.M., & Cryer, D. (1989). *Family Day Care Rating Scale.* New York: Teachers College Press.

Harms, T., Clifford, R.M., & Cryer, D. (1998). *Early Childhood Environment Rating Scale-Revised.* New York: Teachers College Press.

Harms, T., Cryer, D., & Clifford, R.M. (2006). *Infant/Toddler Environment Rating Scale-Revised.* New York: Teachers College Press.

Hinshaw, S.P. (1992). Externalizing behavior problems and academic underachievement in childhood and adolescence: Causal relationships and underlying mechanisms. *Psychological Bulletin, 111*(1), 127–155.

Howes, C., Burchinal, M., Pianta, R.C., Bryant, D., Early, D., Clifford, R., et al. (2008). Ready to learn? Children's pre-academic achievement in pre-kindergarten programs. *Early Childhood Research Quarterly, 23,* 27–50.

Hustedt, J.T., Barnett, W.S., Jung, K., & Figueras, A. (2008). *Impacts of New Mexico PreK on children's school readiness at kindergarten entry: Results from the second year of a growing initiative.* Rutgers University, National Institute for Early Education Research.

Kentucky Department of Education. (2004). *KIDS NOW evaluation project executive summary.* Retrieved May 20, 2009, from http://www.education.ky.gov/NR/rdonlyres/32957A0D-4832-4441-808D-DC1198077206/0/FINALexecsummary20042k.pdf

Kentucky Department of Education. (2007). *KIDS NOW evaluation project executive summary.* Retrieved May 20, 2009, from http://www.education.ky.gov/NR/rdonlyres/C0105037-187D-4874-AB25-B0A0D4989E78/0/KIDSNOWEvaluationProject.pdf

Kentucky Department of Education. (2008a). *STARS for KIDS NOW (quality rating system).* Retrieved May 20, 2009, from http://www.education.ky.gov/KDE/Instructional1Resources/Early1Childhood1Development/STARS11for1KIDS1NOW1(Quality1Rating1System).htm

Kentucky Department of Education. (2008b). *STARS for KIDS NOW child care quality rating system standards: Licensed Type I centers.* Retrieved May 20, 2009, from http://www.education.ky.gov/NR/rdonlyres/14977C21-B550-4B1C-A4E8-91500C7E891A/0/72008TypeIGrid.pdf

LoCasale-Crouch, J., Konold, T., Pianta, R., Howes, C., Burchinal, M., Bryant, D., et al. (2007). Observed classroom quality profiles in state-funded prekindergarten programs and associations with teacher, program, and classroom characteristics. *Early Childhood Research Quarterly, 22,* 3–17.

Lonigan, C., Wagner, J., & Rashotte, C. (2002). *The preschool comprehensive test of phonological and print processing.* Tallahassee: Florida State University.

Lonigan, C.J., Wagner, R.K., Torgesen, J.K., & Rashotte, C.A. (2007). *Test of Preschool Early Literacy.* Austin, TX: Pro-Ed, Inc.

Maryland Child Care Resource Network. (2005). *Child care and early education in Maryland: A guide to Maryland's child care system.* Retrieved April 23, 2009, from http://www.mdchildcare.org/mdcfc/pdfs/childcareandeducation.pdf

Maryland State Department of Education. (2004). *Children entering school ready to learn: School readiness information 2003–2004.* Retrieved April 20, 2009, from http://mdk12.org/instruction/ensure/MMSR/srr.pdf

Maryland State Department of Education. (2007). *Maryland education initiatives.* Retrieved March 28, 2010, from http://www.marylandpublicschools.org/NR/rdonlyres/FCB60C1D-6CC2-4270-BDAA153D67247324/13840/eli_final.pdf http://www.marylandpublicschools.org/nr/rdonlyres/fcb60c1d-6cc2-4270-bdaa-153d67247324/13840/eli_final.pdf

Maryland State Department of Education. (2009a). *2009–2010 Maryland School Readiness Report: Children entering school ready to learn.* Retrieved March 27, 2010, from http://www.marylandpublicschools.org/NR/rdonlyres/BCFF0F0E-33E5-48DA-8F11-28CF333816C2/23495/2010_MMSR_Exec_Summ_Final.pdf

Maryland State Department of Education. (2009b). *Maryland model for school readiness (MMSR): Framework and standards for prekindergarten.* Retrieved April 20, 2009, from http://mdk12.org/instruction/ensure/MMSR/MMSRpkFrameworkAndStandards.pdf

Mashburn, A., Pianta, R., Hamre, B., Downer, J., Barbarin, O., Bryant, D., et al. (2008). Measures of classroom quality in prekindergarten and children's development of academic, language, and social skills. *Child Development, 79* (3), 732–749.

National Institute of Child Health and Human Development. (2002). Early child care and children's development prior to school entry: Results from the NICHD study of early child care. *American Educational Research Journal, 39*(1), 133–164.

New Mexico Early Childhood Education Professional Development. (2010a). *New Mexico Early Childhood Education Career Lattice*. Retrieved March 26, 2010, from http://education.nmsu.edu/projects/cyfd/documents/Prof_Devel_System_ Brochure.pdf

New Mexico Early Childhood Education Professional Development. (2010b). *New Mexico Five-Year Early Childhood Professional Development Plan*. Retrieved March 26, 2010, from https://www.newmexicokids.org/Resource/EarlyCare/ ChildCare/PDFs/ATTACHMENT%205.2.5a%205-YEAR-PLAN%20PRO-FESSIONAL%20DEVELOPMENT.pdf

Pennsylvania Departments of Public Welfare and Education. (2009). *Keystone STARS: Continuous quality improvement for learning programs*. Office of Child Development & Early Learning. Retrieved April 20, 2009, from http://www.pakeys.org/docs/FINAL%202009-2010%20STARS%20 Center%20Standards.pdf

Pennsylvania Key. (n.d). *Early learning in Pennsylvania*. Retrieved April 21, 2009 from http://www.pakeys.org/pages/get.aspx?page=EarlyLearning

Pianta, R., Howes, C., Burchinal, M., Bryant, D., Clifford, R., Early, D., et al. (2005). Features of pre-kindergarten programs, classrooms, and teachers: Do they predict observed classroom quality and child–teacher interactions? *Applied Developmental Science, 9*, 144–159.

Raver, C., Jones, S., Li-Grining, C.P., Metzger, M., Champion, K., & Sardin, L. (2008). Improving preschool classroom processes: Preliminary findings from a randomized trial implemented in Head Start settings. *Early Childhood Research Quarterly, 23*, 10–26.

Rous, B., Howard, M., Chance, L., DeJohn, M., & Hoover, D. (2008). *Overview of Kentucky's early childhood professional development framework*. Lexington: Kentucky Partnership for Early Childhood Services.

Rous, B,. McCormick, K., Gooden, C., & Townley, K.F. (2007). Kentucky's early childhood continuous assessment and accountability system: Local decisions and state supports. *Topics in Early Childhood Special Education, 27*, 19–33.

Shonkoff, J.P., & Phillips, D.A. (2000). *From neurons to neighborhoods: The science of early childhood development*. Washington, DC: National Academy Press.

Smith, M.W., & Dickinson, D.D. (with Sangeorge, A., & Anastasopoulos, L.). (2002). *Early Language and Literacy Classroom Observation (ELLCO) Toolkit* (Research ed.). Baltimore: Paul H. Brookes Publishing Co.

Wishard, A.G.., Shivers, E.M., Howes, C., & Ritchie, S. (2003). Child care program and teacher practices: Associations with quality and children's experiences. *Early Childhood Research Quarterly, 18*, 65–103.

Woodcock, R.W., McGrew, K.S., & Mather, N. (2001). *Woodcock-Johnson III Tests of Achievement*. Itasca, IL: Riverside Publishing.

Woodcock, R.W., & Muñoz, A.F. (1990). *Batería Woodcock-Muñoz Pruebas de Aprovechamiento-Revisados*. Itasca, IL: Riverside Publishing.

Appendix

Ensuring Effective Teaching in Early Childhood Education through Linked Professional Development Systems, Quality Rating Systems and State Competencies: The Role of Research in an Evidence-Driven System[1]

A National Center for Research in Early Childhood Education White Paper

C. Howes, R. Pianta, D. Bryant, B. Hamre, J. Downer, and S. Soliday-Hong

This paper was produced as a consequence of the National Center for Research on Early Childhood Education 2008 Leadership Symposium, held on February 5, 2008, in Arlington, VA. We cannot name all the symposium participants here but rather want to acknowledge their participation and commitment to the discussion and to this initiative for evidence-driven

[1]This appendix is from Howes, C., Pianta, R., Bryant, D., Hamre, B, Downer, J., & Soliday-Hong, S. (2008). *Ensuring effective teaching in early childhood education through linked professional development systems, quality rating systems and state competencies: the role of research in an evidence-driven system* (pp. 1–16). Arlington, VA: National Center for Research on Early Childhood Education; reprinted by permission.

improvements in early childhood education. The research reported here was supported by the Institute of Education Sciences, U.S. Department of Education, through Grant R305A060021 to the University of Virginia. The opinions expressed are those of the authors and do not represent views of the U.S. Department of Education.

Requests for copies of this paper should be sent to Dr. Carollee Howes, UCLA, Department of Education, 3032A Moore Hall, Mailbox 951521, Los Angeles, CA 90095-1521, or additional copies can be downloaded at www.ncrece.org.ncrece national center for research on early childhood education

INTRODUCTION

Policy makers, educators, and researchers have long assumed that a key to effective teaching in early childhood is the professional development of teachers, a process that can span formal educational experiences between high school and graduate school and include formal and informal training and mentoring experiences. One component of this effort to prepare and support effective teachers is state-wide Professional Development Systems (PDS), which comprise the set of requirements and procedures by which states determine who is qualified to teach and the mechanisms for preparing and qualifying teachers. More recent state efforts to improve teachers' effectiveness and classroom experiences for children include Quality Rating Systems (QRS) and statements of Early Childhood Education Competencies (ECEC). QRS are mechanisms for defining the optimal conditions for caring for and preparing children for school, and for encouraging and rewarding improvement to higher levels. QRIS include ratings for continuous improvement as well as rating assessments. Throughout the paper we will use QRS to stand for both types. ECEC are statements that define what teachers need to know and do in order to create optimal learning opportunities for children. PDS prepare teachers for these tasks.

These two additions to the infrastructure for teacher preparation and support, QRS and ECEC, have largely been developed outside of existing PDS. In this paper we argue that PDS have to be better-integrated with QRS and ECEC in order to improve the delivery of ECE services, and we specifically focus on the need for research that documents their integration, linkages, and subsequent effects on teacher performance. Relatively little research has been conducted within QRS and ECEC systems, and even less is known about how they intersect and work together with PDS. It is the intention of this paper to stimulate conceptualization and planning of research on the components of, and linkages among, QRS, PDS, and ECEC, toward the aim of an evidence-driven system through which policy and program development can improve the quality of early childhood services offered to young children.

To put it another way, if we are confident about what teachers need to know and be able to do to be successful in classrooms (ECEC), we can build resources to prepare and support that knowledge and those skills and certify teachers' competence (PDS). We can then put in place accountability mechanisms that spur progress toward higher levels of competence and convey information about competence to stakeholders (QRS). To accomplish this overall aim requires these state efforts—ECEC, PDS, QRS—to be linked.

THE NCRECE LEADERSHIP SYMPOSIUM

This NCRECE White Paper builds on the second annual Leadership Symposium of the National Center for Research on Early Childhood Education (NCRECE) held in February 2008. At this meeting, the invited policy makers, educators, state-level early childhood personnel, and researchers were given the challenge of first defining and describing PDS, QRS, and ECEC, and then creating a set of research questions and proposals that not only produce evidence to support and improve linkages among them, but also assist in building evidence-based systems that integrate preparation, licensure, in-service support, state competencies, and child outcomes into more coherent entities. Three dominant themes emerged from the symposium: 1) PDS themselves are largely non-systems (i.e., most professional development is not systematically linked to teacher, program, or child outcomes), 2) within a given state there are little or no linkages among PDS, QRS, and ECEC, and 3) there is very little consistency or alignment between what is articulated in policy, what is implemented within states or programs (e.g., guidelines activities, approaches, interventions), and what evidence there is that might support those policies or implementations.

It is tempting to look to the K–12 system for knowledge about linkages between professional development and competencies, but there are reasons to believe that this pathway for identifying strategies may not be fruitful. First, ECE historically has been located outside of the K–12 educational system (administratively and policy-wise) in terms of state efforts that focus on teacher qualifications and preparation. There have been only a few successful attempts to align children's learning and development across ECE and K–12 systems, so even at the level of child outcomes there is no coherence or consistency from ECE to K–12. Therefore, the components of ECE systems (e.g., training, curriculum, evaluation) may not match categories typically used in the K–12 educational system. To illustrate, ECE teachers may have either formal education *or* training to be considered effective teachers in some systems, education is as likely to be in-service as preservice, and, in many cases, students receiving preservice in ECE at the 4-year college level never actually teach in the ECE system. Moreover, and perhaps most importantly, there is very little evidence that the questions of relevance in this document about which we might look to K–12 for guidance, such as alignment of teacher competencies and professional development systems, have been addressed in K–12 in ways that produce better outcomes for children or teachers. In fact, recent discussions lament the lack of evidence for teacher preparation in K–12, and the wide-ranging alternatives to address needs of effective teachers suggest that K–12 has had little traction on this complex issue. Therefore, in effect, early childhood education can most likely offer the best solutions for these complex challenges by utilizing lessons learned from the shortcomings of K–12, while recognizing uniqueness and possible assets in domains of teacher preparation and effective teaching.

The symposium discussion drew from a set of presentations by leaders in the field who work closely with state and national policy and program development related to improving the quality of early childhood programs through teacher preparation and professional development. These presentations (*listed at the end of this document and available at www.ncrece.org*) provided both a backdrop for discussions and a set of challenges to symposium participants. Not only was it evident that the field lacks evidence for many policies and state requirements related to teaching (again, not dissimilar to K–12), but that the linkages among state certification, quality rating system metrics, and systems of professional development are virtually unknown, unstudied, and, to the extent that they do exist, unplanned. Notwithstanding these challenges, each speaker argued that the issues of linkage and evidence were central to not only the future development and improvement of systems to support, license, and reward effective teaching, but also to the credibility of the field.

In this NCRECE White paper, we hope to advance the field by outlining the conceptual and evidentiary challenges identified in the symposium and offer suggestions for further study that could be undertaken by individuals and teams of investigators working collaboratively with states and programs. Such efforts, over time, would begin to close the evidence gap and contribute to better policy making. We begin by elaborating on dominant themes of the symposium, the need for more evidence-based approaches within each system, and the need for research on linkages among systems. We describe what is known about PDS, QRS, and ECEC, and identify the overlapping and unique components of these systems. We then describe levels of necessary research: research that defines and describes the components of each "system" and research that can move the field towards an integrated system where PDS, QRS and ECEC are linked in a way that promotes effective service delivery to children.

THE CURRENT STATE OF PROFESSIONAL DEVELOPMENT, QUALITY RATING, AND EARLY CHILDHOOD COMPETENCY SYSTEMS: 2008

To reiterate, the ultimate intent of this paper is to envision state-level systems that link a) what children are intended to know and perform (state learning standards/guidelines) with b) the formal preparation, licensing, certification, and in-service requirements for teachers (Professional Development Systems) and c) approaches to monitoring, incentivizing, and communicating about program quality (Quality Rating Systems), as well as with the expected approaches to instruction and supporting learning that define teachers' practices in relation to state learning standards for children (Early Childhood Educator Competencies). Our argument from the outset is that it makes sense that these elements of a state-level approach to early childhood programming should be linked and that examining linkages and studying effects over time will help states improve policy making and program development. Thus, the symposium and this paper are intended as an initial step in building a conceptual framework and evidence trail in support of a more coherent, unified approach that binds these disparate and relatively separate entities into one system supporting children and teachers.

As a way of depicting our goals and establishing a common framework and lens for discussion, Figure 1 presents a conceptual frame for the discussion and for this report. Readers will see that the three primary foci for policy and program development that states use to ensure effective teaching and effective teachers are depicted as circles (Professional Development Systems, Quality Rating Systems, and for Early Childhood Education Competencies). Paired with each of these foci is a set of specific elements that are actually most often the vehicle for linking corresponding policy initiatives to practice and desired outcomes. The figure also notes the potential of linkages among these three entities (and their elements). Finally, the horizontal line aiming from left to right is intended to reflect that linkages, elements, and foci of policy can change, and through collecting data systematically, such change could be built on the basis of evidence. In the sections to follow, we focus on information presented at the symposium and gathered in the discussions that pertains to establishing this evidence base.

ECE PROFESSIONAL DEVELOPMENT SYSTEMS: THE NEED FOR RESEARCH- AND THEORY-BASED PROFESSIONAL DEVELOPMENT SYSTEMS

A Professional Development System can be defined as having several core components, most common of which are higher education programs that prepare teachers, state and local resources that provide in-service support to teachers through workshops or courses, and a system of licensure and certification through which states use higher education programs and in-service training as a means of certifying teachers as qualified to teach in that state. By this definition, in 2008, according to administrative data, the vast majority of states have some form of a professional development system operating to regulate the workforce in the early education and early child care sectors.

However, these same administrative data suggest that there is highly uneven implementation of PDS across states. To be specific, states differentially regulate teaching staff and various forms of care; that is, they have different qualifications for these roles. For example, in 2006, 78% of the states had preservice higher education qualifications for center directors, while only 25% of states had higher education requirements for center teachers or for large family child care home providers. In short, states often see these roles as very different, when, in fact, each of these individuals is likely to be the primary "teacher" in a "classroom" setting, serving 3- and 4-year-olds; and, not surprisingly, these requirements differ from state to state.

Even when states require some level of preservice preparation in higher education for entry into a professional role as a teacher, there is, in general, a low level of preservice qualification required for licensure or certification in early childhood. For example, Child Development Associate certificates are the most common preservice requirement for directors and master teachers in early childhood education programs, while experience alone or together with a high school diploma is the most common minimum preservice requirement for teachers. Only 40% of state PDS require a preservice course on working with children with disabilities, and only 10% require a course on working with children learning English as a second language. Thus, apart from the background of variability in entry qualifications into various roles, compared with K–12, there is a rather low level of entry qualifications as well.

State professional development systems tend to put more emphasis on in-service training than preservice qualifications for continued licensure, with 46% of states requiring ongoing training for center teachers, 40% for center directors, and 36% for small family child care providers. This emphasis on on-the-job training (in contrast to preservice training as noted above) places the burden of workforce quality on state and local systems of in-service support, rather than on state institutions of higher education and its well-established infrastructure and capacity. With regard to the primary point of this discussion, if states were to move to better exploit the capacity of higher education institutions in their approach to licensure and certification in all the varied roles in early childhood education and care, it would be imperative to make very close connections and linkages among teacher preparation in higher education, statements of teacher knowledge and skills competencies (ECEC), and standards for child outcomes.

A central issue throughout this discussion is the extent to which data are available on the linkages of interest—in this case, between professional development systems and ECEC, that is to say, between degree status and teachers' knowledge/skills in competencies needed for certification. For the most part, states do not collect the type of information needed to examine this connection (this being a reason for the widely noted lack of association between a BA degree and classroom quality). State administrative data collected as a part of PDS typically document how many early childhood program staff have participated in various sanctioned training activities (e.g., courses) and at what level (e.g., AA, BA). However, we know little about how PDS are working or what impact they have had on the ECE systems; states do not have information on individuals' training, licensure, certification status, and knowledge and skills in the classroom. Rather, states certify higher education and in-service programs on the basis of mapping coursework and fieldwork onto state competencies and assume that individuals who progress through these training and preparation experiences have the desired knowledge and skills.

Another issue with regard to professional development systems, particularly for ongoing training and in-service support, is the extent to which teachers and providers make use of resources when they are available. This is key to understanding and using PDS as a mechanism for improving teaching in ECE. For any improvements in effective teaching, teachers and providers have to be motivated and provided with opportunities to participate in professional development. In the field of early childhood education, low compensation and recognition often interfere with teachers' and providers' motivation and opportunity to engage in professional development. It has been suggested by proponents of Quality Rating Systems that by directly assessing program quality and linking helpful resources and training requirements to those assessments, such systems have the potential to confer an incentive on teacher to participate in in-service training and support. The need to facilitate teachers to participate in PD would also give programs and incentive to provide supports for PD, such as paid time off for required PD activities, and sponsorship of PD attendance (e.g., pay for workshops, hiring internal coaches, providing substitute teachers, etc.). Again, this suggests an important link between states' Professional Development Systems and QRS that should be made explicit and studied.

A final, and particularly important, consideration concerns the type and intensity of professional development that may be necessary to create and sustain changes in teachers' practice. Thus, although the vast majority of PDS focus on coursework and workshops as the primary vehicles for preparation and training, we now know that the daily interactions that teachers have with children are critical to children's social and academic development, and we are just learning how to go about changing these interactions. We need more research in this area in order to more effectively support our teachers and improve student outcomes. Recent research suggests that targeted intervention into teacher interactions with children and instructional climate for academic skills such as the *MyTeachingPartner* work by Pianta and colleagues can increase effective teaching and children's academic gains (more information can be found at www.myteachingpartner.net). Other evidence, such as the QUINCE project by Bryant (2007) and colleagues, suggests that ongoing mentoring and consultation increases effective teaching. Mentoring and training are very difficult to measure and to bring to scale, though relatively "easy" to prescribe as the professional development answer. One critical component of bringing mentoring to scale concerns the ability of systems to prepare and regulate mentors, yet only three states have defined core competencies for technical assistant providers.

In sum, there is a clear and compelling rationale for state PDS (e.g., preservice and PD in the context of higher education programs, in-service training, licensure and certification requirements) to be closely connected to the descriptions of state competencies and the systems of monitoring and incentives that can be used as leverage to improve program quality and child outcomes.

ECE QUALITY RATING SYSTEMS: MEASURING TEACHER EFFECTIVENESS, CLASSROOM PROCESSES, CHILDREN'S OUTCOMES

Quality Rating Systems fundamentally are mechanisms for defining the optimal conditions for caring for and preparing children for school and for encouraging and rewarding improvement to higher levels. They provide a way to open the system of early childhood programs to market-based forces (e.g., consumers of child care have information on quality), and they offer a variety of mechanisms for states to define levels of quality and desirable outcomes for the programs in which they invest, which, in turn, become markers for monitoring and resource allocation. Mitchell (2005) has written extensively about QRS, and they are featured in the Pew Early Childhood Accountability framework.

Since the 1990s, the number of states with QRS has grown and systems have evolved in several ways. No longer funded solely by state-level sources, many initiatives are now funded through multiple sources, including foundations. The diverse funding sources for QRS may bring multiple and diverse requirements, affecting how these systems change. Although intended to apply to the entire range of early childhood programming (family-based child care, formal and informal settings, center-based preschools), another development is the increasing participation of state pre-kindergarten programs in QRS. Originally designed to guide consumers (e.g., parents), QRS now are driving changes in ECE programs, especially in professional development requirements.

As has been mentioned, states vary considerably in whether they are adopting a QRS, the components of the QRS (classroom observation, child outcomes, teacher qualifications, etc.), and the specific metrics the states extract from these components and the definitions for identifying a "quality" program. For example, for states in which classroom observation might be a component, states may vary on the nature of the observation system used and the actual levels of scores obtained from that use, as they identify classrooms that meet or do not meet certain standards. Every one of these decisions could be informed by data as the systems are constructed, but more important are the data that could be collected as systems are implemented and refined, so that they are improved in terms of efficiency and effectiveness over time.

For example, states using QRS could pool information on their components, metrics, and definitions for quality, and comparisons across states could inform efficiency and resource planning as states learn from one another about costs, staffing, and how metrics perform in the field. Furthermore, if a given state(s) gathered information on teachers' professional development experiences as a function of QRS, and the costs and returns of that professional development to quality and child outcomes (or ECE competencies), then the QRS, as a system for monitoring and incentivizing program improvement, might be fine-tuned over time to align more closely with effective professional development opportunities.

In many ways, QRS should function as a mechanism for linking professional development systems and states' lists of competencies for early childhood educators. In theory, the QRS monitoring systems would include valid measures of competencies that would also be reflected in the coursework and training offered to teachers through higher education and local/state in-service offerings. Again, we argue that the linkages among these systems are critical if any one of them is to achieve its potential for improvement of programs across a state.

The Maine Roads to Quality Registry is an example of a statewide effort to link teacher qualifications and training to early childhood competencies (Mayfield, Mauzy, Foulkes, Dean, & Foulkes, 2007). Teachers who join the registry receive a registry certificate, a registry transcript, career counseling, and eligibility for other programs, including scholarships. The Maine Roads Core Knowledge Training Program is an affiliated 180-hour training program that is aligned with Maine's K–12 Learning Results, with accrediting and legislative requirements, and prepares teachers to work with children according to the competency priorities of the state. Maine is an example of one of several states, including Missouri, Montana, and Wisconsin, that joined the National Registry Alliance to develop best practices for data collection systems which are exemplars of designing mechanisms for documenting and encouraging improvement and defining the optimal practices for preparing children for school.

ECEC: WHAT DO ECE TEACHERS NEED TO KNOW AND DO?

ECE competencies are what ECE educators need to know and do to demonstrate that they are well prepared to effectively educate and care for young children. Clearly, there are a host of knowledge domains as well as skills that could be included in these systems, and often there are multiple layers of organization in ECE competency lists. ECE competencies typically start with broad concepts or domains of knowledge and skill (e.g., knowledge about child development, working with families). Within those broad domains are clusters of specific knowledge areas and skills. For example, the domain of *Knowledge about Human Growth and Development* could include clusters of knowledge areas pertaining to cognitive development, social development, or physical growth and development, with each one of these areas then broken down into specific information (e.g., understands pathways of syntactic development or understands role of attachment in emotional development). Similarly, in broad skill domains (e.g., working with families) one might find a cluster of skills around "transition planning with families" that could then be defined in terms of "plans and implements effective transition plans with parents." Thus, a key aspect of ECEC systems and lists is this multilayered organization of knowledge and skills and the very large range and number of units within each layer. Their very complexity is often an impediment to their utility.

Interestingly, unlike K–12, for which all states have lists of teacher competencies for knowledge and skills, only 26 states have competency standards for early childhood educators, with similarities across states. For those states with competencies specified, across states there is wide variation in the number of levels and content of each level. Moreover, most states map these competencies onto various forms of certification, licensure, and roles within the ECE workforce, and again there is considerable variation in this mapping. Some states organize competencies by titles (director, teacher, aide), some by degree (CDA, AA, BA, MA), and some by levels on a career ladder. By and large, there is very little evidence to inform this mapping process, and often it can seem quite arbitrary. There is little evidence to drive decisions about what a teacher needs to know and do that is separate from a teacher's aide, for example, and even less evidence that ties specific knowledge or skills to a specific degree, in terms of how that combination of knowledge/skills and degree or role is critical for advancing the quality of the ECE programming offered in a state and in child outcomes.

More important for the focus of this paper is the need for linkage between state competencies and the systems on which states rely to produce those competencies (PDS), and for the systems to monitor, make them public, and align them with outcomes (QRS). A critical issue for linkage is the level of detail or specificity at which linkage is sought: For example, do QRS operate to ensure "knowledge of cognitive development" or "skill in transition planning" through direct assessment of teacher knowledge or observation of skills, which would be linkage at a rather specific level, or through some check-off stating that the teacher took a course with that title, a rather general level of linkage? Furthermore, the lack of assessments available for many of these knowledge and skill domains, which could be used as metrics in a QRS or as drivers for designing professional development opportunities, is a major impediment to the efficient and effective use of state competencies as a mechanism for the improvement of early childhood programs. Our ability to develop research- and theory-based ECE competencies is limited by our lack of reliable and valid assessments of teacher knowledge. The development of such a measure would greatly enhance our ability to connect the field and reduce the complexity of this problem.

How best to provide the resources needed to ensure that teachers have these competences is not yet known. Even at entry level, what a teacher needs to know is substantial. Assuring that the competencies address a wide range of issues is challenging—they need to address cultural and linguistic diversity, be applicable to infants through eight-year-olds and to family child care providers as well as classroom teachers, and include knowledge and skills related to special needs children, to name a few such issues.

WHAT DATA ARE BEING COLLECTED AS PART OF THE IMPLEMENTATION OF QRS, COMPETENCY SYSTEMS, AND PROFESSIONAL DEVELOPMENT?

To study the integration of these three systems, it is important to assess the data being collected as part of the implementation of QRS, competency standards, and Professional Development. The short answer to this question is that, within a state, almost no data are collected in the same way across systems, and what data are being collected is very different across states. Moreover, given turnover rates of personnel across the system, data quickly become outdated.

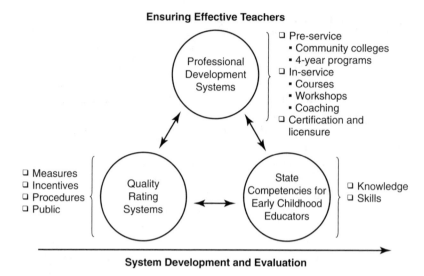

Figure I.   Ensuring effective teachers.

Figure 1 notes the main focal areas of each of the three systems and the major domains from which, if consistent data were available, we would be better positioned to understand and enhance the integration of systems.

However, as States become more proficient in collecting and making administrative data accessible, such data can be useful in addressing preliminary descriptive questions. Likewise, as national efforts are launched to capture and make equivalent data collection efforts across states, these descriptions can be made on the national level. Examples of such efforts are described in the next section.

Within the state competency area, teacher registries are the best example of the data typically collected. A teacher registry is a local, state, or national database that gathers listings of teachers and their certification or professional development. Registries exist in 28 states. They are a good source of data to track the content of teachers' training and education, and some track the competencies of the trainers of ECE competencies. The National Registry Alliance has developed core data elements to address cross-state consistency in definition and measurement in teacher registries. Cross-state consistency allows for tracking of professional development on a more national level and benefits teachers who have a resource to document their qualifications to current employers and to bring their credentials with them, should they move across states. Finally, teacher registries allow stakeholders to better understand the connection between teacher education, training, experience, and outcome measures, such as teacher turnover and alignment with early childhood standards.

The National Association of Child Care Resource and Referral Agencies (NACCRRA) conducted a survey focusing on training provided by CCR&Rs to approximately 500,000 providers, teachers, and administrators (Smith, Sarkar, Perry-Manning, & Schmalzried, 2006). The survey distinguished between discrete workshops and sequenced workshops and asked about the qualifications of those providing the training and the content addressed by training. NACCRRA is currently piloting an extension of its software program (NACCRRAware) to include ongoing documentation of Training and Technical Assistance. This is a promising step in the direction of linking professional development opportunities (e.g., course and workshops) to the individuals enrolled in these opportunities, which could serve the purpose of helping determine whether these opportunities are effective. However, a periodic survey, such as this, is not as useful in terms of tracking exposure and effects as a registry and had as its purpose the linking of individuals to training opportunities and enrollment.

Within the QRS area, the data collection systems underlying QRS are a source of information on various features of early childhood programs/services (e.g., teacher/child ratios, class sizes, observations of classrooms) and the professional development experiences and credentials of ECE staff, usually all staff in a program. Across states, QRS data vary with the elements of the system. QRS administrators and researchers often find it efficient to examine QRS data, but these databases do not meet all needs. For example, for technical assistance purposes, a behavior-specific measure is useful, but that level of specificity may not be needed for other purposes. As a particular example, many QRS systems use the Early Childhood Environmental Rating Scale ECERS (Harms, Clifford, & Cryer, 1998). While individual ECERS items or subscale scores may assist programs in quality improvement for research purposes, an overall score is more meaningful.

Overall, QRS procedures also vary on how data are collected, whether by outside independent observers or self-report measures. Relying on teachers and caregivers as a source for information of their own behaviors is problematic. This is particularly true when the measurement carries high stakes with it. For example, if teachers' or programs' funding is dependent on high QRS scores, the only sensible strategy for teachers is to rate each child as competent and each classroom as high in quality.

There are other measurement issues related to the constructs assessed in QRS. First, relatively easy structural measures that serve as markers of quality in QRS (formal education, credentials, training, certification) may not indeed measure effective teaching or quality ECE programs. Increasing research evidence suggests that these markers by themselves do not map onto children's academic readiness for school (Early, et al., 2006,

2007). Furthermore, evidence suggests that the context of the teaching interacts with the professional development of the teacher (Howes, James, & Ritchie, 2003; Vu, Jeon, Howes, 2008). That is to say, it is unlikely that a constrained set of professional development experiences will help all teachers equally or meet the diverse needs of teachers working in increasingly diverse settings.

Second, it is difficult and expensive to measure what may really matter to children's academic readiness for school, though certainly possible. Classroom observations may be critical to the process of improving ECE settings, given the unreliable connection between more readily available data (e.g., teacher education, rations) and child outcomes. Observational assessments are difficult to implement, especially at the scale required for this endeavor, requiring considerable resources for training observers and traveling to conduct classroom observations. However, the types of teacher–child interactions that are associated with student outcomes cannot be self-assessed by teachers. Thus, including observation as a component of QRS is an expensive venture.

A third challenge for QRS data is the reliability of the data that are collected. A fair and credible system of accountability is required. Are observers and portfolio raters trained and reliable? Can we guarantee teachers and programs that they will get the same ratings, regardless of who comes to perform that rating? If child measures are part of the QRS, are they collected by independent, certified assessors or by teacher report? If by teacher report, how well are the teachers trained? Validity and cultural appropriateness of measures are concerns. For a QRS, or for a QRS to translate into improvements in children's social and academic development, we need to pay attention to how closely aligned the components of the system are with child outcomes. Are the observational measures used global quality ratings or specific teaching strategies? Is there evidence that links the measures to children's preacademic success? Given the diversity of early childhood programs, QRS also need to be concerned with the extent to which measures are appropriate to the cultural and linguistic diversity of the children and families in the system. We do not have good measures of culturally responsive pedagogy and family/community support. Better articulation of the outcomes we desire in family support practices and cultural competency is needed, as well as more specificity as to which teachers should be responsible.

THE BARRIERS TO INTEGRATION OF SYSTEMS

The preceding section noted several differences between the data available from PDS, QRS, and ECEC systems, differences that make it challenging to integrate the systems. Other barriers to integration exist. States tend to regulate programs rather than having a PDS; that is, states require ECE programs to hire teachers who have certain numbers of courses or, in some cases, a degree. State institutions of higher education at the 2- or 4-year level may offer courses or degrees, but these are not necessarily matched to regulations, QRS, or explicitly to ECEC. In addition, training is often disconnected from education, typically because training and technical assistance are provided by state or local agencies (e.g., CCR&Rs), which are not part of institutions of higher education and which do not align their professional development with community colleges and universities. The largest part of the burden of PDS falls mainly on these agencies, and they typically provide PD via workshops, mentoring, and consultation. There is no regulation of the quality of this PD or the extent to which it is aligned with the other systems. In addition, as with teachers, there is high turnover of trainers and TA providers.

INTEGRATING THE THREE SYSTEMS

Ideally, the integration of these three systems would be based on a logic model that is empirically informed, provides explicit rationale for linkages among the systems, and ultimately results in children's positive development. Proposed steps in this logic model are outlined as follows:

1. The foundation of an integrated system should be children's early learning standards, defined in accordance with, or elaborating on, existing early childhood performance standards (e.g., Head Start, NAEYC) and in collaboration with the K–12 system.

2. Then, a set of Early Childhood Educator competencies needs to be developed that encompasses the knowledge and skills necessary to help children learn the skills identified in the preestablished early learning standards, as supported by recent research. What do teachers need to know and be able to do in classrooms that promotes children's learning?

3. Next, both preservice and in-service Professional Development experiences need to be developed to address these research-based core ECE competencies. Efforts must be made to empirically examine professional development experiences, whether a college-level, semester-long course as part of a degree program or an in-service mentorship program, and determine which PD experiences actually result in teacher development among the ECE competencies and which experiences may be most helpful for teachers. This ongoing process will lead to the availability of a dynamic, ever-growing suite of PD resources/experiences with known links to ECE competencies.

4. Then, Quality Rating Systems need to be designed so that they directly measure the teacher knowledge and skills that are listed in the core ECE competencies and that are being taught and supported through available PD systems.

5. With all of the systems aligned in the aforementioned manner, QRS data can then be utilized in at least three different ways to solidify linkages across the three systems:

    a. As an accountability mechanism, QRS data can be used to ensure that ECE competencies are related to children's learning in expected ways.

    b. As a slightly different accountability mechanism, QRS data can be used to ensure that teachers experiencing certain types of PD are making expected improvements in ECE competencies.

    c. As a feedback mechanism, QRS data can be used to identify teachers who are struggling with specific ECE competencies and link them with a PD experience that addresses these competencies.

    + dev. PD to address this

WHAT STUDY DESIGNS COULD EVALUATE THE INTEGRATION OF PROFESSIONAL DEVELOPMENT INTO QRS AND COMPETENCIES SYSTEMS?

The symposium participants worked in small groups to expand and elaborate the constructs needed to better study the three components of the system. (See Table 1 for a complete list of constructs developed.) We concluded that within-system questions (e.g., Does some form of PD work?) as well as cross-system questions (e.g., Are PD and QRS aligned and, if so, to what effect?) could form the basis of new research projects. In this section of the paper, we use the constructs and designs generated by the participants to craft a framework in which individuals in a particular agency can locate their work within the whole system and perhaps begin to address gaps in the system. We also attempt to delineate some of the important research that should be conducted.

Although, as we have discussed, data collection efforts are uneven, using existing data are most desirable in terms of cost. However, due to the concerns mentioned earlier, any data collection effort will probably need to collect new data. This is an understudied area and there are essentially no data comparable across states. Nor is there standardization of definitions, terms, elements of systems, categories of children/families served, parts of workforce covered, and perhaps more.

Research could be conducted *within* a state to better understand its own system and *across* states to better understand PD/QRS systems, and,

Table 1. Constructs and Their Components

Construct	Components/Issues
Child	What is the age range of children included in the system? Are the systems adjusted to be appropriate for children in different age groups (e.g. toddler vs. school age) Are child outcomes in synchrony with ECE competencies, PD, and QRS?
The workforce	What is the scope of the workforce included in systems? For example, is it only people in direct instruction and care, or does it include support staff (e.g., nutritionists, those providing transportation)
The setting	Which settings are included in systems? For example, are family-friend and neighbor care included? Are we including only people who accept payment for their services or others as well?
Professional development system components	How does the state define the workforce (i.e., degree, credential, certificate)? Does formal education include both degree and major? Is course content embedded within degree program (e.g., course at community college vs. course in BA program)? Is the course part of training equivalent to a college credit course? Is the course preservice or in-service? Can an assets approach be used (i.e., participation in professional meetings, participation in intensive training (sequenced sessions), discussing professional progress, having a support person visit the program)?
Quality and accountability in PD training	Are the PD trainers certified? Is the course curriculum codified? Has the training program been evaluated?
Context of teaching	What is the form of care? Is there more than one adult in the classroom? Is there supervision? Is there mentoring? Is there accountability? What is the infrastructure of support for teacher?
Program support	What are the program administrator's education, training, skills and experience with supervision?
Families and children served	Maternal education, income level, ethnicity, home language, immigrant status
Baseline of PD infrastructure, by state	Is there integration of state learning standards and ECE competencies? What is the role of higher education in ECE PD? Are the ECE competencies integrated into coursework?
Trainer	What is the range of skills? What are the levels of practitioners trainers are qualified to train?
State licensing system	What is the basis of licensing regulations? Does licensing vary by funding stream?
Subsidized child care system	What is the interrelation between subsidies and QRS-based reimbursements?
Capacity and sustainability	Do QRS systems create programs that are available to all families? Does the capacity of the system remain the same after improvements? Are the systems sustainable? What is the capacity of the state to continually support systems?
Child	What is the age range of the children included in the system? Are the systems adjusted to be appropriate for children in different age groups (e.g., toddler vs. school age) Are child outcomes in synchrony with ECE competencies, PD, and QRS?
The workforce	What is the scope of the workforce included in systems? For example, is it only people in direct instruction and care, or does it include support staff (e.g., nutritionists, those providing transportation).

ideally, both types of research would be funded. States with more advanced and linked PD data systems can assist states beginning to create or change their systems, although context (e.g., population density, poverty levels) might lead one state to address a particular issue in a different way than another.

DESIGNING RESEARCH. SEVERAL TYPES OF STUDIES WERE DISCUSSED BY SYMPOSIUM PARTICIPANTS

A validation study within a particular state, especially one with data in each of the three domains discussed here, could test the linkages between the hypothesized connections—for example, more training leads to better quality teaching, which in turn leads to better children's outcomes. Such a study would need the cooperation of the various agencies that were the gatekeepers of the data and probably some third-party linking of identifiers, but it would allow examination of some of the assumptions. Similar studies replicated over several states or communities would be even more instructive. Several relatively small-scale validation studies of PD systems would be useful if the researchers were particularly careful to nest the validation within a described context (e.g., child income and ethnic background, sector of care [FCC, Pre-K, etc.], infrastructure support).

Another type of design is a logic model and literature validation study (or studies) based on a small number of states to describe, through stakeholders eyes, what they intend to do (logic model), the dimensions they have selected into their PD system, and the literature that supports the inclusion of those dimensions and the logical links between them. This work would use the existing evidence base for the dimensions and for the desired outcomes of those dimensions.

A third type of study discussed by participants consisted of descriptive studies that could document the variations in PD systems across states and communities and the various levels of integration of PD into ECE competencies and QRS that are found. This kind of study, which would need to go beyond surveys in order to capture the complexity and commonality (or not) of the various systems, would include any or all of the following:

- Case study comparisons of the integration of PD into QRS and ECE competencies in a small number of selected states.

- The use of ethnographic methods and open-ended questions to interview teacher participants, higher education faculty, and trainers.

- Observation of the implementation of selected PD and QRS using ethnographic descriptions.

- The use of NCRECE measures of teacher knowledge, teacher performance, and child outcome as validation instruments for a selected number of teacher and classrooms in each state.

Finally, although expensive to conduct, larger scale studies that might incorporate the dimensions and variations of all three systems would allow all the links in the chains to be assessed. Data from such studies could be used to focus on the dimensions that are shown to be most important for quality outcomes or children's outcomes, to set the gradations of PD or QRS systems more evenly, and, ideally, to trim the amount of data needed to the essential elements that account for the most variance.

CONCLUSION

This symposium and the development of the White Paper have highlighted both the promise and the short- and long-term challenges of research designed to examine the interface between PD, QRS, and ECEC systems. The first step in such a research program is measure development. The logic model and validation research designs described herein as first steps in this research process require careful definition of constructs and their operational definitions in administrative data. Furthermore, measurement development must be completed with attention to the context of teaching and to definitional discrepancies and commonalities within and across administrative and research data. We recommend that requests for proposals be issued by public and foundation funding sources to complete these tasks of measurement development. We further recommend that once reliable and valid measures are in place, a series of small-scale studies be undertaken to describe these systems and their overlap. Finally, any hard conclusions about the efficacy of such systems, their interface, and their influences on teaching practices and children's development await large-scale studies that include direct independent observations within classrooms and family child care homes.

REFERENCES

Bryant, D. (November, 2007). *Delivering and evaluating the Partners for Inclusion model of early childhood professional development in a five state collaborative study.* Presentation at the meetings of the National Association for the Education of Young Children, Chicago, IL.

Early, D., Bryant, D., Pianta, R.C., Clifford, R., Burchinal, M., Ritchie, S., Howes, C., & Barbarin, O. (2006). Are teachers' education, major, and credentials related to classroom quality and children's academic gains in pre-kindergarten? *Early Childhood Research Quarterly, 21*(2), 174–195.

Early, D. M., Maxwell, K. L., Burchinal, M., Alva, S., Bender, R., Bryant, D., Cai, K., et al., (2007). Teachers' education, classroom quality, and young children's academic skills: Results from seven studies of preschool programs. *Child Development, 78*(2), 558–580.

Fukkink, R.G., & Lont, A. (2007). Does training matter? A meta-analysis and review of caregiver training studies. *Early Childhood Research Quarterly, 22*(3), 294–311.

Harms, T., Clifford, R. M., & Cryer, D. (1998). *The early childhood environment rating scale* (Rev. ed.). New York: Teachers College Press.

Howes, C., James, J., & Ritchie, S. (2003). Pathways to effective teaching. *Early Childhood Research Quarterly, 18*(1), 104–120.

Maxwell, K. L., Field, C. C., & Clifford, R. M. (2006). Toward better definition and measurement of early childhood professional development. In M. Zaslow and I. Martinez-Beck (Eds.), *Critical issues in early childhood professional development* (pp. 21–48). Baltimore: Paul H. Brookes Publishing Co.

Mayfield, W. A., Mauzy, D., Foulkes, T., Dean, A., & Foulkes, M. (2007). *State of the Maine Registry* (Policy brief). Columbia, MO: Center for Family Policy & Research, University of Missouri. Accessed Online July 9, 2008 at http://muskie.usm.maine.edu/maineroads/pdfs/Maine%20Policy%20Brief%201.23.07.pdf

Mitchell, A. (2005). *Stair steps to quality: A guide for states and communities developing quality rating systems for early care and education*. Alexandria, VA: United Way Success by Six.

National Registry Alliance (January, 2006). National Registry Alliance core data elements: Achieving consistency among member states. Available on www.registryalliance.org/Resources and Policy Briefs/Cove Data Elements.pdf

Smith, L. K., Sarkar, M., Perry-Manning, L., & Schmalzried, B. (November, 2006). *NACCRRA's national survey of child care resource and referral training*. Arlington, VA: National Association of Child Care Resource and Referral Agencies. www.naccrra.org

Vu, J.A., Jeon, H., & Howes, C. (2008). Formal education, credential, or both: Early childhood program classroom practices. *Early Education and Development 19*, 479–504.

Index

Page references followed by *t* or *f* denote tables or figures, respectively.